A SAILOR'S GUIDE TO
REGATTA
PREPARATION

A SAILOR'S GUIDE TO REGATTA PREPARATION

FOR BETTER RESULTS IN DINGHY, KEELBOAT AND ONE-DESIGN RACING

Mark Chisnell

To Phil and Sasha

Copyright © 1996 by Mark Chisnell

First published in the UK in 1996
by Waterline Books, an imprint of Airlife Publishing Ltd

British Library Cataloguing in Publication Data
A catalogue record for this book
is available from the British Library

ISBN 1 85310 543 0

Typeset by Servis Filmsetting Ltd, Manchester
Printed in England by Biddles Ltd., Guildford and King's Lynn

Waterline Books
an imprint of Airlife Publishing Ltd
101 Longden Road, Shrewsbury SY3 9EB

Contents

Introduction

This book is intended for anyone who wants to take their regatta sailing seriously. You might be the club champion or a regular winner on the local open meeting circuit and fancy a crack at the National Championships. Or you may already have a couple of Nationals under your belt and be wondering how to pull yourself up into the top ten, and from there go on to the World Championships. These pages are intended to give a clear insight into the level and type of preparation necessary to compete and win at the big events. Much of what is here is applicable to a wide range of classes, from dinghies through to keelboats and small one-design yachts.

It is a trend of the past two or three decades that, with the sport becoming more sophisticated, the literature has become increasingly specialist. We have gone from the era of John Oakley's all encompassing *Winning*, through Dave Perry's *Winning in One-Designs* to arrive at Lawrie Smith's *Tuning for Yachts and Small Keelboats*, each title narrowing its attention as it becomes more difficult to cover the entire range of available knowledge in one volume. To go on to write a book covering the full spectrum of racing topics may seem to be perversely bucking a trend for which there are good reasons. But it is because of the present nature of the bookshelves' offerings that a broader work like this seems necessary. Few campaigns have unlimited amounts of time and money, and so the most important skill is to prioritise correctly between the competing demands on your resources. Otherwise too much attention to one area will lead to a critical failing in another.

The intention is that this book will form a blueprint for your approach to a championship regatta, guiding and advising on all aspects from getting to it with the car and the boat intact (and several people have not) to having the right accommodation when you arrive. After reading this book my hope is that through an appreciation of what would be the perfect regatta preparation, you will be better able to balance your own approach. So when you do have to compromise you can do so understanding the consequences and in the area that is least likely to affect your overall performance.

In attempting to cover such a broad range of subjects in a limited space there will inevitably be omissions. It is not the intention in the section on boat speed, for instance, to try to rewrite or replace other excellent works on boat tune. But adequate (or better) boat speed is an essential part of the preparation we are talking about. What will be discussed is how to approach achieving it, rather than specific advice on which string to pull and when. Part of doing that job is for each chapter to recommend further books that will provide more detailed and more expert advice on the separate topics.

Part 1 is certainly the most important section. It concerns all the elements that must be in place before you even think about going near the water, your own approach and objectives, your mental and physical fitness and skills, choosing and keeping a crew, and similarly selecting and defining the relationship with a coach. If these elements are not in place before you start sailing the rest of the book will be of limited value – because no amount of boat preparation, sail testing, venue research, and efficient logistics will save a campaign that is structurally wrong from under-performing. And it will be structurally wrong if you have the wrong attitude, have picked the wrong goal or have the wrong crew or coach. Only when you have assimilated the lessons of Part 1 will the rest of the book have any solid value.

Finally I should like to thank Rob Andrews for his help in both clarifying the thoughts that went into Chapter 1 and providing much of the material for Chapter 3, as well as reading the original manuscript. What finally made it on to the page, with any errors and omissions, is of course solely my responsibility. My thanks also to Peter Bentley for providing the photographs and to those who gave permission to use copyright material.

MARK CHISNELL

Part 1

People Preparation

Chapter 1

The Individual

The season is over, your sailing has gone reasonably well, but the result you were looking for at the National Championships has eluded you. As the nights draw in, the memories fade of that final race when the week's inexorable slide out of the top ten became a freefall. The wind is howling outside and a succession of dartboard-like weather systems has kept you off the water for weeks. You sit down in front of the fire one December evening with a blank sheet of paper and start to plan. Next year will be different, you are going to have the perfect regatta campaign. Now, where do you start?

The first place you start is in your own head. Do you have the right attitude to be a winner? Or is everything you do, every penny you spend, every minute you practise or work on the boat undermined by the most fundamental thing of all – your inner self? Yes, would have to be the answer in ninety per cent of the population. Mind-set, mental attitude, whatever you want to call it, is the principal limiting factor in most people's sailing performance. And if you have never considered it before, then do so, because it is your best hope of improvement. Better than buying new sails or a new boat, or practising heavy-weather gybing for a whole week. If you get your head right, everything else will follow.

So before you jot down on that piece of paper who your boat builder or sailmaker or crew will be, consider two things, your approach and your goal.

A Professional Approach

There is much talk in sport of professionalism, and the term has come to mean more than whether or not someone gets paid. A professional approach is regarded as essential to success in modern sport – but what do we really mean by a professional approach? A professional approach is a state of mind, an attitude that pervades everything you do in connection with the sporting endeavour. I think it can be characterised by three key elements: control, a positive attitude, and personal responsibility (I am grateful to Rob Andrews for this breakdown).

Control

It is important that you are aware of what you can control and what you cannot, and even more important that you do not worry about things that are beyond your control. This includes many of the things that sailors are most susceptible to getting wound up about. You cannot control the fact that there is a postponement because there is no wind, or that the race officer has left the last leg as a fetch instead of re-laying the marks to give you a proper beat and a better chance to catch up. Nor can you control the guy in the black boat who has just slammed on your air for the fourth time today, despite the fact he is thirty places behind you overall. You cannot control the umpire who has just called you up on an infringement at a mark rounding that you were clearly not guilty of. If you allow your rage and frustration at these events to take over, you will perform badly, and for what reason? None at all, there was nothing you could do about it. So why worry?

You can, however, control the equipment that you are sailing with, the number of hours you have spent maintaining it, the number of hours you spend training and whether or not there is a good weather forecast on the boat. If you can control it, do so, make it happen the right way. Imagine you are at the big regatta with a group of your friends. You have all been training together for the last few months and the conditions have always been windy. You all have great confidence in a breeze now and as a consequence you are all fast. The day of the first race dawns and the wind is barely stirring the cobwebs in your light airs inventory. But the race committee gets a start off and you have a shocker. But so do all your friends. That night in the club the talk is pervasively gloomy: everyone's slow, the forecast is for light airs all week, couldn't get a shift right, it's hopeless . . . But you need not be dragged down by this: remember, you can control who you talk to. Leave your friends in their slough of despond, find someone you know who had a good result. Talk to them about how they set their sails up and trimmed them, did they think there was a pattern to the shifts, what was their strategy, how are they going to play it tomorrow? Let some of the radiance of their success rub off on you.

Positive Attitude

You should look upon any events in the campaign with a positive attitude – weaknesses in your performance are not cause for despondency, but golden opportunities to improve. If you are slow sailing upwind in light air, great; think how much better you will do when you have cracked the problem. Take a positive attitude to solving it, find the people who are fast and copy their settings, set yourself the goal of developing more light air boat speed and work out a programme to achieve it.

Personal Responsibility

It is your campaign, your regatta and your performance. Ultimately only you are responsible for what happens. You must be the one that takes the decisions and controls your own destiny. Certainly you should listen to ideas, advice and comments, from coaches, crew and even competitors or friends. But when faced with several options you are the one that has, and makes, the choice. And you must also accept the responsibility when it is the wrong one. Blaming external factors or other people's decisions for the outcome of your regatta is a negative move that will do nothing for a future improved performance. Only by accepting personal responsibility will you become aware of your own strengths and weaknesses and be able to distinguish between those things that you can do something about and those that cannot be altered. Once you have accepted this you can take responsibility for working on those weaknesses, establish your goals and set the agenda to achieve them.

Goal Setting

We have already mentioned goal setting several times, and next to acquiring a professional attitude the most important mental skill is the setting of realistic, achievable goals. On that windy December night you are doing just that, setting your regatta goal for next year. That is a long-term goal, but equally important are the short-term goals that you must set on the way to achieving it. But let's talk about the long-term goal first.

The key words when it comes to goal setting are 'realistic' and 'achievable'. And what is realistic and achievable will depend on two things, the current stage of development of your ability and the resources of time and money that you have available to you. The first thing you must decide is what resources you have to commit to the campaign. There is no point setting an Olympic gold as your target if you can afford no more than a few weeks and a couple of thousand pounds as an operating budget a year. You must set the goal to match realistically the resources that you have. Trying to achieve things that you are not prepared to make the sacrifices for, or do not have the resources to fund, can only lead to unhappiness.

To win an Olympic medal in the 1990s and beyond requires nothing less than a full-time commitment, along with access to thousands of pounds a year to fund the effort. Winning a World Championship in an Olympic or top international class requires not much less. Even a National Championship is unlikely to be won with less than every weekend and most evenings of the week being devoted to the cause. Ask yourself how important your sailing is to you. Is it the most important thing in your life, in which case nothing less than Olympic glory will satisfy, or does it come down a little bit, after family, friends, and perhaps your career?

You must also be realistic in your appraisal of your current level of ability. If you have just championed your club for the first time, then a World Championship win next season is probably beyond you – but top ten at the Nationals should not be. So let us assume for the moment that your goal is just that, a top ten Nationals position, something which should be achievable by most successful amateur sailors. You have already come up against the first problem in using goal setting in sailing. The only measure, or perhaps I should say the most obvious measure, of success is the result. And that is something that you cannot control; you have no idea how everyone else is going to sail. You may well be capable of a top ten position, but if twenty other people sail an absolute blinder all week, however close you sail to the limits of your ability you will not get a top ten position.

Other sports are much better placed with regard to this. How often have you seen an athlete come off the track after placing sixth or seventh and say, 'Delighted with the performance, knocked half a second off my personal best, fabulous effort, really pleased John'. They have a definitive measure, in time, of their performance. Perhaps the track or the weather conditions have a little bit of impact on it, but not much. In sailing we have no such luxury. Somehow out of the phenomenal variety of performance indicators and variants we must pick one that measures all these complex variables, and we find . . . the result.

Perhaps this is acceptable in terms of our eventual goal. Results are, after all, how everyone else will measure us, the media, friends and family, our peer group. And perhaps at the end of a long campaign it should come down to where you finally finished. Sports psychologists are still arguing over this one. But there is little doubt that results-based goals are particularly destructive in the short term. Realism and avoiding results are the dominant factors when setting your short-term goals.

The first thing you need is a comprehensive assessment of your own ability. There are various ways of going about this; you can do it formally or informally. Which approach you take will depend on how good you are. If you are an inland club sailor and are tackling your first open water

Technical Evaluation

Technical Areas:

	Importance for next Training Period	Current Performance	Their Best Performance
Hull (including fairness, gaskets etc.)			
Foils			
Sails			
Choice of Jibs			
Spinnaker			
Boat preparation			
Tuning Numbers/Settings			

Sailing Areas

Acceleration (from start)			
Tacking			
Gybing - reach to reach & run to run			
Mark Rounding			
Starting			
Pressure Boathandling			
Waves Upwind			
Waves Downwind			

Tactical Areas

Rules			
Percentage sailing			
Covering			
Boat on Boat			

Strategic Areas

Meteorology			
Currents/tides			
Great escapes (set moves)			
Compass/shift work			
Protest technique			
Extreme Options			

RYA Technical Evaluation Form, reproduced with permission of the RYA.

championship it is pretty clear where your weaknesses will be; wave sailing, big fleet starts and tidal strategy for starters. If you are at Olympic level and looking for that final half a per cent to drag you into the medals then a more refined, formal approach may be necessary. Reproduced on page 19 is an example of the RYA's technical evaluation forms for their Olympic squad.

Each of the topics is judged by the sailor under the three headings, marked out of ten. The topics themselves may be modified by the individual, hence the jargon. 'Pressure boathandling' is boathandling under stress from the racing situation, and 'Great Escapes' is not the movie, but what these sailors regard as set-piece tactical moves to extricate themselves from a bad position – stuck outside eight boats at the gybe mark, buried at the start, and so on.

In this case your current performance compared to your best performance allows you to see the weaknesses and to judge how important work in that area is to the next training session. It is possible to refine this idea further. Each topic is assessed as to its importance to the campaign. Then your own ideal ability in that topic is assessed, followed by your current level of performance, all three being marked out of ten. So let us imagine we are 470 sailors assessing Starting. On short courses we regard this as 10 for Importance. We also adjudge 10 to be our Ideal Ability Level on the start line. Finally we assess our Current Level to be 5. Now we want to calculate what we will call the Priority Factor. This is our Ideal Ability Level minus our Current Level, the result multiplied by the Importance. So for starting our Priority Factor is given by:

$$\text{Priority Factor} = (10 - 5) \times 10 = 50$$

The higher the Priority Factor, the higher your priority to work on that area should be! The advantage of this system is that when you assess all the different areas with it, the weaknesses really leap out at you because of the multiplication involved. Try it and see. It is a good exercise to see if the results agree with your own more informal assessment of your abilities and weaknesses.

Once you have assessed where your problems lie you have to figure out how to work on them. Let's take the start as an example. The first job is to break down what skills are involved in starting. This will depend on the type of boat: with a big heavy keelboat the most important thing will be time and distance judgement so that you hit the line at full speed; with anything lighter and smaller different skills will be at the forefront.

The 470 is a good example. The skills necessary for getting off a crowded line are the ability to accelerate the boat and have complete control at close quarters and slow speeds in difficult conditions of wind and water. You also need a good spatial awareness – who is around you and how fast they are moving as well as where the line is. So now you can break this down even more. How long does it take you to accelerate the boat from a standing start in five knots and ten knots of windspeed? Try and see, then watch someone who is a good starter do it and see how long it takes them – your first goal is to match their time. Watch other starts and see what the techniques are; the double tack to move you off a boat that is too close to leeward, sailing the boat out of a stall, stopping it in its own length, moving to windward or leeward without moving forward. All these boathandling techniques can be broken down and analysed. Then all you need to improve them is a fixed mark, a stopwatch, and some old sails.

When you feel you have a definite improvement it is time to set yourself some regatta goals. You may have been PMS'd three times in your last regatta; try and get through the next one cleanly. If you achieved it, how much worse were your first windward mark places? Were you depending on a jump at the start to get a good first beat? If so, maybe you need to work on first beat strategy and tactics a little more if you cannot give yourself that starting edge legally. If you are buried on most start lines, go to a regatta aiming to be PMS'd three out of six times, find out what it feels like to have your nose clear, find how much harder you could have been pushing it without getting caught.

For this exercise to work you have to be honest with yourself about where you stand now and what you need to work on to achieve your final goal. It is easy in a book like this to slip into a hypothetical world of infinite resources. That exists for none of us, so choose what you can do, which areas will provide the most efficient return on time, money and effort carefully. Once you have done this you need to develop a programme of intermediate goals and the necessary practice and preparation sessions that will allow you to achieve them. You must always be reappraising the situation, assessing where the present problems are, where the most gains are to be made.

We should consider what to do if the whole thing starts to go off the rails. Perhaps the time and effort you thought you could commit for some reason does not become available. Perhaps the carefully organised practice does not produce the results; you are continually falling short of the goals you have set yourself. What then? Personally I believe that failure at a goal is no major thing. Okay, so you only managed two good starts out of six; if the regatta before produced zero then you have improved. Perhaps you schedule in a couple more training sessions focused on starting, and keep starting on your list of goals for the next regatta. Maybe a secondary one, but still worthy of attention. Move on to the next item on the list, don't get too locked up on one thing. Desperate repetition and effort at one particular aspect often has a negative effect overall. Maybe you move starting down to a months time for a review. You will be surprised how often, by the time you get to the review stage, the problem has disappeared. You have quietly assimilated and applied the skills so assiduously practised without noticing.

Mental Skills

We have talked a lot about two central mental skills, the professional attitude and goal setting, and I think these are fundamental to your regatta preparation. And I think that if you work with these two basic plans you will build a solid base to launch your quest for regatta success. There are a whole group of other more specific mental skills that you should also be aware of when you are preparing yourself for racing. Because it is in the mind that most championships are won and lost. We have all seen examples, whatever level we sail at. The regatta favourite who blows the first couple of races, then when the event is effectively over and the chance of winning overall is gone, suddenly comes good and blitzes everybody in the last two races. Or the underdog who comes from nowhere to lead overall after three races – then disappears to mid-fleet. Or the club sailor who, despite years of sailing, seems unable ever to get up there and actually win a prize. But of course there are many more famous and more public examples in the true spectator sports. Anybody who watched Roberto Baggio blast his penalty over the bar in the 1994 World Cup Final shoot-out knows something about sports psychology. Baggio was fighting the same battle with a recalcitrant conscious mind that you are doing as you weave in towards the gybe mark, leading a hundred-boat fleet in twenty knots. How do you avoid his mistake?

Much as you train your body to be fit enough to race you can also train your mind to improve skills and deal better with the stresses it will be subject to out on the race course. There are lots of different techniques, some are simple and others are very sophisticated. But you need not consult a sports psychologist to benefit from these things. Some of the ideas you may already be using without realising that they are established sports psychology techniques.

One of the most common, and something that you often see mentioned by competitors in different sports, is that of mental imagery and rehearsal. You think through difficult manoeuvres (gybing in a breeze) or tricky stages in the race (second row on the start line) and imagine yourself sailing your way out of trouble smoothly. Psychological research has shown that imagining yourself gybing, tacking and starting perfectly is the next most effective way to practise it, behind being on the water actually doing it. Imagining the perfect heavy weather gybe reinforces in your mind the movements and reactions. So sitting on the beach thinking through the smart moves you will soon be making on the start line is one of the best ways you can prepare for the race. And a recognised mental training technique.

There are other techniques to deal with different aspects of the race. Stress management and relaxation techniques, such as centring, teach people how to cope with pressure. Allowing them to focus back on the race and stop getting locked onto a single destructive thought – such as how badly your crew did that last gybe. Other techniques will improve your concentration, build and maintain your confidence and get you fired up again when you start to lose interest and the will to win. These are critical skills to competitive racing, and unless you are the type who can naturally focus on the job for a whole race, taking upsets in your stride and never letting the pressure get to you, you should work at mental training.

There are two particularly good books for more information on this topic. *Mental and Physical Fitness for Sailing*, by Alan Beggs, John Derbyshire and Sir John Whitmore, published by Fernhurst, deals specifically with a wide range of mental training techniques and how to apply them. Eric Twiname's *Sail, Race and Win*, recently rewritten by Cathy Foster, also deals extensively with developing a winning mental approach. Both are strongly recommended.

Physical Fitness

Along with preparing your mind comes preparing your body, but if the former is under-emphasised then the latter is all too often over-emphasised. Perhaps this is because society generally has become rather obsessed with fitness and diet. We are deluged with fitness issues on tv, and in magazines and newspapers, and it is easy to reflect this knowledge in our sailing preparation. But time spent on unnecessary physical training is time wasted – the type of bad prioritising that we want to avoid. You only need train to the level required for the boat you are sailing. For the tactician aboard a keelboat this might mean no training at all, unless you lead a particularly sedentary life outside of your sailing! For a Laser sailor aiming for Olympic gold this probably means two or three hours in the gym every day, all of which should be carefully programmed and monitored.

To judge your level of fitness you need to know whether

it is detracting from your performance. Think about the last time you sailed in a breeze – what were you thinking about on the last beat? How to get to the finish line faster, or the pain in your legs? If it was the latter then your fitness level is certainly detracting from your performance. Your fitness should allow you to complete all the physical tasks aboard the boat you are sailing without affecting your concentration. If it is not, then you need to take some action to improve it. Tiredness at any part of the race will affect your concentration, and this can only slow you down.

So what sort of training should you undertake? Again it depends on the type of sailing you are doing. For less demanding keelboats and dinghies, maintaining a reasonable level of aerobic fitness is probably enough. Playing a sport two or three times a week should be sufficient. This is a matter of personal taste; squash, football, running, swimming and cycling will all provide aerobic fitness. Mixing them up will stop you getting bored.

For those people sailing high performance boats with a big fitness demand, something more specific will be required. *Mental and Physical Fitness for Sailing*, listed previously, provides an excellent general review of the subject along with specific advice on exercises for different types of sailing. The other possibility is joining a gym and finding an instructor who will help you sort out an exercise routine to work the specific muscle groups that you are using. But if they know nothing about sailing, you will have to explain carefully the type of work you are doing on the boat, to get the right exercise programme.

It is easy to get sucked into the training-for-its-own-sake cycle though, and to end up working far harder at your fitness than you need to. This over-emphasis on fitness will only detract from your sailing – you could be spending that time and effort on other more productive aspects. The fitness is a means to an end – getting round the race-course without running out of steam – not the end in itself.

Chapter 2
The Crew

We have talked about your plan for the season, the campaign programme, and if you sail a singlehander then you are the only person that you have to consider. But if you sail anything bigger then your first task in fulfilling your plan will be finding the crew. It may be that you already have a crew; perhaps you have sailed together for years and you are planning to move on to your new goal together. If this is the case you should take a long look at the basis of your relationship in the boat, and decide whether or not it will stand up to a tough championship regatta campaign.

There are two reasons people sail together: firstly, friendship; and secondly, because the boat's programme matches the personal goals of the individuals. The higher the level of competition that you aim at, the more you need a crewing relationship based on the latter rather than the former. The reason for this is that the more intense the competition, the greater the demands on everyone involved. The boat's programme will have to take priority over many things: friends, families, careers, other hobbies. When the pressure comes on, you will find that friendship is not a good enough reason for meeting the demands being made. If that is the sole reason you are involved, then you do not honestly believe in the value of the goal

Once you have achieved it, the satisfaction of sailing as part of a top-flight crew will never be forgotten. (*Peter Bentley*)

that you are striving for. But if you do believe in the goal, and share the ambition, then you will be prepared to make the sacrifices. It is not necessary for the personal goals of each individual to match exactly, so long as they collide in the agreed regatta programme of the boat and are held with equal conviction and willingness to make sacrifices. The brilliant eighteen-year-old helmsman may want to win the Puddle Creeper OD national championship because he wants to be the next Lawrie Smith, and he knows Joe Bloggs the sailmaker will give him a job that will start him off as a professional if he does. The twenty-seven-year-old crew member may want to win it because he's been second three times already and has promised himself one more, full-bore go at it before getting married in the autumn. The important thing is that both agree to the regatta aim and commit to it and the necessary sacrifices equally.

Of course, finding the right person is not going to be easy. It is perhaps the hardest part of any campaign. And the more ambitious your goal, the more difficult it will be to find the right person to share it. It is hard enough in this age of diverse leisure pursuits to find someone to turn up every Sunday morning for a season's club racing, but all weekend and most week nights as well? Unless that person truly shares your ambition and is prepared to commit to it with a passion equal to your own, the relationship will not work. The fault line in any crew always runs down the point where ambition and commitment do not match. As long as they do, and both feel they are getting what they want out of the deal, the boat will work. If they do not, then the whole thing falls apart.

Crewing relationships are like any other kind, you have to work at them. And people are only prepared to work at something when they feel they are getting commensurate rewards for their effort. Winning a regatta they do not care about will not be viewed as reasonable reward for the commitment of every second of their leisure time. And as soon as someone starts feeling like this, they stop working at the relationship and it collapses. For this reason it is often worth finding a crew with less sailing ability, but which is prepared to match your commitment, than the other way around.

Where does that leave friendship? As a worthwhile but inessential part of the crewing relationship. Although shared ambition, rather than friendship, is the reason you are together, life is a lot more pleasant if you sail with someone whose company you enjoy during those long hours on the championship trail. And a long campaign, particularly one that includes time away from home, training or competing, is smoothed by a certain amount of social compatibility. But I repeat, it is not essential. I have seen boats sail fast when the crew ignored one another from virtually the moment they completed the debrief until the next time they went afloat.

So, whilst personal compatibility is a worthwhile trait in a crew, it is not a performance priority. What are the other factors to be considered should you find yourself in the fortunate position of having a choice of crews with equal commitment? A crew's ability to do the job has two main components, skill and physical build. Both of these can be worked on, skill levels by training and practising, and physical build through exercise or diet, but a basic deficiency in either will leave you struggling.

Some research amongst the successful sailors in the class will tell you the ideal crew weight. Keep in mind that mobility, height and build are also considerations in the more physical boats. Don't underrate this factor if you are new to top flight campaigning. A serious excess or lack of weight (5 to 10 kgs outside the parameters) will find you struggling in one wind condition no matter how good you are. Also give yourself the opportunity to make a proper judgement about a potential crew's ability. Take them out for a trial sail or race to see how you get on together in the boat. Make sure you put them under pressure, both in technique and decision-making, to see how they react.

You should also consider (and if the above has not given you a clear candidate by now, you are spoilt for choice) what type of skills and commitment the other person can bring to the campaign. If you drive the boat fast but are tactically naive, then you probably don't want a crew with similar preoccupations. If you have a tendency to crack under pressure, finding someone who is particularly cool for the front of the boat will obviously be a bonus. Equally, if you can bring plenty of funds to the campaign, but only a minimum amount of time because of a demanding job, then it may not work out if you sail with someone who has similar commitments.

Having the opportunity to consider these last factors before you choose a crew is a bonus. But even if your short list has come down to one, long before you got this far in the selection process, a frank discussion of the division of responsibilities and roles is your next task.

Collective Responsibility

Once you have found a crew the next stage is to define the relationship as carefully as possible, and this means both in and out of the boat. The first thing is to divide the various responsibilities for preparation. This is where the shared level of commitment comes in. If one of you is doing everything – funding the campaign, the boatwork, organising the travel and accommodation – whilst the other just turns up, it will be almost impossible to prevent resentment from building between you. The closer your contributions are, with whatever resources you have, the longer the campaign is likely to last. One of you may have more time, the other more money. These commodities, at least as far as sailing is concerned, are directly convertible (though the exchange rate can float unpredictably). Let whoever has the money foot the bills, and whoever has the time do all the running around, organise and do the boatwork.

The more you can talk through this issue early on, the easier it will be down the track when the pressure starts to build. If you really can contribute no more than just turning up at the regatta venue, say so; give the other person a chance to find someone else, don't promise commitment you will not give. A common example is the helmsman who is desperate to get a top-flight crewman for his campaign, and in trying to encourage him aboard promises him the earth: 'I'll do everything, pay for everything, just turn up, that'll be fine'. Initially this arrangement might seem acceptable. The crewman is contributing a wealth of skill, experience and reputation the helmsman does not have, in exchange for the helmsman providing everything else. But this type of deal can so easily go wrong, particularly if handled badly by the crew.

Imagine mid-season approaching, and the helm is disappearing under a mountain of conflicting pressures of family, finance, boat maintenance and work problems. He has been hassled by the wife, kids and the boss all week, been in the garage trying to sort out the new spinnaker halyard retrieval system till midnight the day before and then got up at five that morning to drive to the event. Stuck in traffic he's an hour late at the venue; not seeing his crew, he frantically rigs the boat. It's the final qualifier for the Worlds, they need a good result or the whole season's wasted; he glances at his watch, half an hour to the ten! Then he sees the crewman strolling down towards the boat with a new girlfriend on his arm and a relaxed and cheery grin on his face. How would you feel? The relationship is unlikely to survive. As a helm in this situation you are much better off finding someone at the beginning of their sailing career, perhaps like yourself, burning up with energy and ambition, who will match your commitment hour for hour, pound of flesh for pound of flesh.

Contract

Although it sounds tedious there is a lot to be said for writing this down, defining the relationship on paper. It doesn't need to be a contract (unless it is a particularly professional campaign with a lot of money and prestige at stake), just a list of who is responsible for what. This can be carried to quite a degree of detail, and aboard a yacht might become a complex affair. You must define who is responsible for everything – packing sails, doing repairs, running the work list, entering, reading the sailing instructions, provisioning the boat, and so on.

The simplest way to start is for each individual to take the responsibility for his area. The sail trimmers, for instance, will ensure the right sails are on the boat and that any necessary repairs or modifications are done. Those forward of the mast will ensure that the sails are packed properly both in their bags and on to the boat. The crew boss will be responsible for running a work list of jobs that need doing to the boat and checking that someone does them. Overseeing all this and making sure that it happens is the skipper. It is his job to ensure that everyone understands their role and that nothing is either left out or done twice.

Checklist

When I am sailing as a navigator I use a list of items and tasks that must be checked before the boat goes sailing. Sometimes the jobs overlap with the responsibilities the tactician might take upon himself, but I'd rather see something done twice than not at all. Sitting down and talking through who is doing what will save the work being duplicated. I have reproduced this list below as an example of the kind of attention to detail that is necessary aboard a yacht on a big campaign. Everyone involved should have a similar assessment of their responsibilities.

Checklist; Navigator

1. All race course charts listed and filed below in a waterproof area
2. Tidal Information (current/tidal atlas and high water times)
3. Waypoint List (offshore only)
4. Sailing Instructions and Notice of Race
5. B, I and Class flag, any other?
6. Declaration
7. Protest form
8. Rule Book
9. Any Special Safety Regulations Navigation Requirements
10. Hand-held VHF (charged?)
11. FM, AM and Long-Wave radio
12. Radio Forecast List (Times and Frequencies, for VHF, radio and weather fax if carried on board)

13. Latest Weather Forecast
14. Are all the electronics working and calibrated?
15. Equipment Manuals
16. Spares
17. Navigation Equipment (parallel rule, dividers and pencils)
18. Binoculars
19. Wetnotes and Pencils
20. Hand Bearing Compass
21. Polar Table and Target Speeds
22. Calculator, Ready Reckoners or Computer

Whilst immeasurably simpler, the division of responsibilities aboard a dinghy can be less obvious and so it is just as important to sit down, talk it through and perhaps write it down as well. An example of why this is worth doing occurred during 470 sailing prior to the Olympic trials in 1992. Emerging, on most occasions, from the changing room after my crew I would find him talking to someone, while the boat languished unready to launch. I would then spend another five minutes putting what I felt to be the necessary finishing touches before the boat went down the ramp. Five minutes later in the launch queue could easily turn into twenty minutes later on the water at overcrowded facilities, with a corresponding increase in the stress level of the helmsman.

The cause of the problem was that we had completely different ideas of what constituted 'ready to launch'. We talked it through and came up with a list of jobs that had to be done each morning before the boat was ready to go. Only then could either of us take time out to chat to our friends. It included everything from getting the weather forecast and checking the noticeboard for amendments, to taking the rudder blade cover off and tying up the cunningham on the boom. The transformation at the next event was remarkable. Despite my repeated tardiness in the changing room we were always ready to hit the water early and could then devote our time to distracting others from their more hurried preparations.

Respect

The other dimension to any sailing relationship is what goes on on the water. What you most need is respect for each other. This may come as a matter of reputation, prior to your teaming up. It may come through sailing together. But when you have it, it will provide you with the right atmosphere to get on with the job. Each crew member will trust the others to do their jobs properly and will let them get on with it. When something goes wrong there are no accusations flying through the air. Those nearest the error are allowed to deal with it, because the others trust them to be the best people for the job.

The flip side to this situation occurs when that trust and respect does not exist. What usually happens then is that there is a fight to establish a pecking order, and the most obvious symptom of this is a lot of 'point-scoring', by which I mean that everyone is always looking to establish themselves by scoring points off other members of the crew, by spotting and pointing out their mistakes. Of course this concentration on other people's tasks rather than their own leads to their own performance being sub-standard, which in turn gives other people the opportunity to score a few back from them. This then further incenses that individual, prompting him not to perform better but to find more of the other's mistakes. And on it goes in a vicious circle of deteriorating performance.

If you come into the programme with a level of mutual respect for each other, the situation is unlikely to deteriorate in this fashion. If a group of diverse people is brought together to sail, especially on a bigger boat with more crew, then this is a much more likely scenario. Once again the way round this is communication, by establishing the pecking order and responsibility right at the start and, as the season develops, using the forum of a debrief run by the skipper to make changes. This maintains the discipline and does not allow anyone to think they can jump up the pecking order, and so encourage them to have a go at other people on the boat.

So when you bring a crew together, be it two or twenty people, divide the tasks, both general and specific, on the water in exactly the same way as off the water. You can decide who is responsible for making the final call on tactics and trimming. More specifically, you can agree exactly who does what on each manoeuvre. On a big boat this will obviously be more complex than for a dinghy, but it is equally important for both. And once you have a system that works you should not change it – at least not outside a crisis. If everyone does the same job every time, things will go smoothly. And when they do not, when someone is suddenly forced out of their position through injury, gear failure or an abnormal situation, the rest of the crew will be able to cover that much more easily because they know exactly what tasks the missing person is not doing. The crew will move smoothly to cover for them, dividing the extra responsibilities with just a few quiet words between them. I have seen boats where disasters have been so effectively dealt with by the foredeck that the afterguard didn't even know something had gone wrong until they were told about it in the bar afterwards.

Practising

The final stage in crew preparation is practising, putting into effect everything you have talked about and planned, and making it all work. What you practise and why is discussed elsewhere, so I just want to make a couple of comments here about getting crews together to practise. The most important thing about crew practice is to remember that other people's time is precious. It is essential that you have planned how you will spend the hours on the water beforehand and that the whole session is run efficiently. There is nothing worse than dragging people out to practise and then wasting their time because you have forgotten the rudder or the key to the boat, not bothered to check whether there is access to the slipway, or the club launch is running and so on. The bigger the crew, the more important this is. Some of them will be on the periphery of the project already, and if you start wasting their time, morale and interest will sink fast.

As it will if the session is not made interesting for everyone involved. Hours of straight line tuning may be great fun for the helmsman and possibly a trimmer, but for cold trapeze crews with cramp, or rail fodder on Bmax, it quickly loses its charm. But at the same time try not to get sucked into the boathandling practice trap. It is easy to over-emphasise boathandling as it is physical rather than mental fitness. You go out for the afternoon and because you have the crew there you think you must do crew work. The result is going through the motions with a few manoeuvres and thinking you have achieved something. The time might have been much better spent on speed testing, time and distance and acceleration work, and so on. Ask yourself, how important is boathandling to the regatta? If you are getting together a match-racing crew for a year on the circuit, then boathandling is funda-mental to your expectations of success. If you are getting a crew together for a season of offshore racing then boat-handling will be well down the list of priorities.

I must confess that I tend to regard boathandling as an inconvenient distraction from the real issues, although I hasten to add that I am not a match racer and I am fortu-nate enough to sail with crews who for the most part take boathandling for granted. Sure, it helps if you shave off a couple of seconds with every mark rounding, but if it takes you a week of solid practising to achieve this, you have to balance it against what else could be achieved with that time. And I think in most other areas of the sport you could achieve more. So if you can get round marks and through tacks and gybes in a tidy fashion, leave it at that. If you are still fouling up sheets and dropping sails in the water, work on it.

Chapter 3
The Coach

Coaching means, and is, different things to different people. What you want and can get from coaching help will depend on the standard of your sailing. For most people, 'coach' brings up the idea of the guy in a rubber boat with a loud hailer telling you to ease the cunningham and move forward a bit. Certainly, this kind of coaching is useful, particularly if you are trying to make the first jump from club level up into national competition. But it has its limitations; most obviously you have to believe that the individual telling you to let the cunningham off is right. And the better you get, the fewer people there will be in whom you have this faith, and the more expensive it will be to get those people to help!

But the coach can and quickly will take on an altogether different role, which Rob Andrews (coach to World Championship-winning 470 sailors and windsurfers) defines as a facilitator: a person that makes things happen, creates an environment in which success comes naturally. Supplying logistic support to the programme is one such task for a facilitator. There are, as you will see in the remaining chapters of this book, a huge number of jobs to be done throughout a campaign. It is easy for the skipper to end up responsible for all these and consequently to disappear in a mound of detail and paper work.

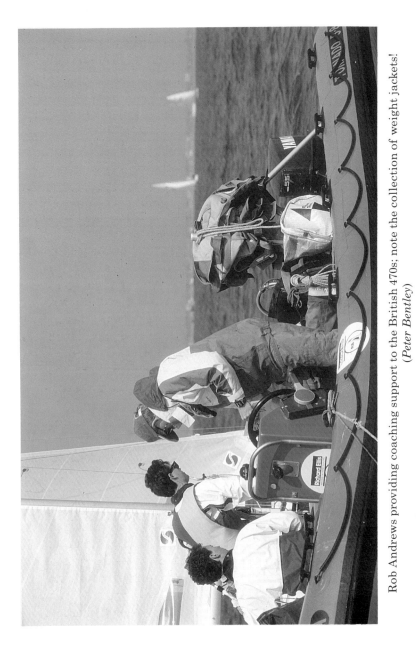

Rob Andrews providing coaching support to the British 470s; note the collection of weight jackets! *(Peter Bentley)*

You cannot sail well if your mind is not clear and focused on the job. The coach can supply the manpower to book the ferries, accommodation, entry, pick up the new sails, the lunches and so on. When your boat fails to weigh in at the World Championships (which it shouldn't) it needn't be you rushing around in thirty-five degrees centigrade looking for some extra lead to screw in and getting totally stressed doing it, it can be the coach.

If you have access to some kind of powerboat and the coach is able to get onto the water with you then there are other jobs to be done. There are extra or spare sails to be carried out onto the water, along with tool kits, warm clothing, food and water – all the things you may need during a day's racing or training but do not want to clutter the boat with. With a little explanation and practice almost anyone can take some useful video or still photography footage. Taking shots of you or others sailing, showing sail trim and balance, tacking or gybing techniques, does not need anything more than photographic knowledge. All it requires is a careful explanation from the sailors about the angles and type of photo you are looking for.

So, fulfilling this kind of role does not require any sailing experience – just a methodical individual taking a disciplined, 'professional' approach. Your partner or another family member or friend could provide this kind of coaching support. But even if they are not involved in the racing be careful with regard to family members, because objectivity and sensitivity are vital coaching attributes. There is a famous story of a British Olympian who decked his brother with a single blow after a less than tactful remark. But the classic, unobjective, over-emotionally involved family coaches are probably parents who, regardless of how little or much they know, insist on rushing along the water's edge screaming advice at their offspring. And you do not see such behaviour from just family members either: apoplectic football managers foaming at the mouth on the touchline are a world and code-wide phenomenon. It goes without saying, then, that if you are to take on someone as a coach, particularly if they are involved in anything more than just logistical support, you need to be very clear what you, and they, are doing. But if you have the right person then their input can be invaluable. Here is a third person, involved but with a much more objective viewpoint of the whole campaign, who can advise on all those aspects of the race and the programme that the sailors are too involved to see clearly. Much of what we discussed in Chapter 1 becomes simpler with a good coach.

This is particularly true of the analysis of strength and weakness and the subsequent goal setting. Out on the water a knowledgeable, uninvolved pair of eyes is priceless. Anyone who has watched a sailboat race will know how much clearer it all is from the outside; everything from sail trim to tactics can be seen by a good observer in a mobile boat. Post-race debriefs can become that much more effective when conducted by an observant coach.

A coach can provide that objective measure of improvement, the 'personal best' we so desperately need in sailing. He can pull out from your nightmare race the forgotten fact that you actually did have a good start, which was what you were there to practise. He can provide dispassionate comment on both good and bad elements of the performance, suggest new methods or prepare training sessions to work on weaknesses. In a crewed boat he can be a crucial mediator. A step back from the action, he can facilitate the right atmosphere for improvement and success. At the very top level the coach will be comfortable with all elements of the programme, and if he does not know the answer he will source someone who does. It may mean setting up sessions with a sports psychologist for a helmsman who's a 'shouter'. It may be finding a yacht designer to refine rudder shape, it could be digging up a marketing company that will help in the search for sponsored finance. But as well as all this the coach will be there at those crucial moments, when you have just had your brains blown all over the water in the first race of the championship and your crew has made repeated calls to go the wrong way. You know he's feeling bad, you know he just had a bad day, you know deep down that you could not have done any better. It was just one of those days. But you are seeing months of effort and practice slip away and the red film of anger will not subside. You cannot bring yourself to speak to him as you drag the boat up the beach. The coach walks up to you – what will he say? If it's the right thing it will diffuse the situation and put you back on the path to a normal performance tomorrow. If it's the wrong thing it could destroy your whole week.

The coach, then, is in a powerful position. His is a job which, if done well, can be a highly positive contribution to the campaign. But if done badly it can do just as much damage, so engaging a coach is not to be done lightly. Even if they are around just to smooth the logistical path they must understand some of what the game is about. And if they are to provide a full coaching role you should ask yourself, are they as professional about their coaching as you are about your sailing? If the answer is anything other than 'more so', find somebody else.

Part 2

Boat Preparation

Chapter 4

Boat Maintenance

The old and clichéd adage, that you don't win races sitting on the beach fixing your boat, has the redeeming feature of being true. When it comes to getting the boat round the track in one piece there is no substitute for preventative maintenance. Whilst you may be prepared to accept a certain amount of gear failure at club or open meeting level when the stakes are not too high (in exchange for more time on the water rather than in the garage working on the boat), any failure at a championship regatta will make it hard for you to achieve your goals. And if you are inclined to be a little bit slack on it for the rest of the season, remember that a bad failure at the beginning of a weekend's club racing or practice can lose you the whole two days' sailing. So at all stages, boat maintenance (as opposed to rigging new systems) should have a priority.

You must be organised about this: keep a work list for the boat at all times. In particular, establish a system for recording equipment problems on the boat. Then you can note them down, if not while you are racing, at least as soon as you cross the finish line. It is easy to find something that is not quite working during the race, but to have completely forgotten about it by the time you reach the dinghy park or the marina. On a dinghy this is perhaps most easily done with a chinagraph or grease pencil on the sidetanks (sticky-backed Velcro is ideal for securing the pencil somewhere so that it is always to hand); in anything bigger a set of wetnotes (waterproof paper notebook and pencil) is invaluable.

Before Leaving for the Regatta

When you come to the regatta itself, in addition to ensuring that the work list is completed, you should conduct a thorough check of the boat and all its gear before you leave. Examine all fittings to see that they work and are properly secured to the boat or mast. In the case of cam cleats this means checking that they spring open and shut properly. If they are not working, it is often just a case of washing them out and then spraying a light oil inside. But it is fairly common to break the spring in the cam, so that they do not close by themselves, and these can often be replaced individually. Check that the jaws of all types of cleat do not allow the rope to slip because they are worn. This is the type of problem that can appear when the wind is strong, after a few weeks of light air sailing, and everything is loaded up that much more. You do not want that to be the first race of the championship, so check the cleats by trying to pull ropes back through them. If you have any suspicions, replacement is the only safe option.

All the blocks and pulleys should be carefully examined to ensure that they are running freely. Again, do this with the pulley under load, as split ball-bearings and worn sheaves sometimes do not appear until the block is stressed. Do not forget static high load attachments, such as shroud bases and the mast step fitting. There should be no movement in any of these. The same goes for all the rudder fittings from the tip of the blade

Serious gear failure will almost always end your regatta hopes. (*Peter Bentley*)

to the end of the tiller. Check the bailers and hatch covers close properly and do not leak. Is the non-slip still living up to its name?

Check the mast for any sign of cracks or fatigue on the section, or any attachments such as spreaders. If you see anything you are worried or are not sure about, check it with the mast manufacturer or dealer. Look for broken or bent strands in wire rigging, and terminations that are damaged in any way. Rig failure is almost always catastrophic to your regatta hopes and you should have complete confidence in the mast and everything holding it up. All other wire and rope on the boat should be examined in the same way, wire for broken strands and damaged terminations, ropes for chafe and wear.

This check should ensure that when you arrive at the venue you do not lose any sailing time to boat maintenance that could have been completed beforehand. Time at the venue is too important to waste on that, unless of course you have factored it into your plans. If you are departing England in the middle of winter to do a regatta in the south of France, it may well be more sensible to leave a couple of days early and do the boatwork down there in the sunshine, rather than in some freezing shed or garage. But only if you know that you will have access to any spares you might need once you get down there. This also assumes that no damage is done in transit, which cannot always be taken for granted.

Getting There Intact

Your boat will almost certainly get to the venue in one of three ways: on a container ship, sailed on its own bottom, or by car, either trailed or roof-topped. Completing this process without disaster can be harder than you think.

The horror stories are many – the three containered German FDs that went off the deck of a ship on the way to a World Championship is perhaps the best known. But I've lost count of the number of boats that have ended up in various states of disrepair on the sides of European motorways. Whilst there was not much the FD sailors could have done, there are precautions you can take.

If you are trailing the boat make sure both the car and the trailer are up to it. The car should be recently serviced and be powerful enough to pull and, just as importantly, to stop the trailer. Getting to the bottom of a hill with your heart in your mouth and the brakes on fire is not a good start to the regatta. The trailer should be strong enough for the job, and you should always carry a spare wheel and bearings. If you are packing gear in the boat make sure the weight is forward, because if you make the nose too light the trailer will have a tendency to snake – and you could end up losing control of the car.

Just as important a consideration when packing gear in the boat is the boat itself. Most of the damage to a lightly constructed racing hull happens when it is being trailed. Packing a lot of heavy gear, such as tool boxes, on the unsupported bottom of a boat sitting on a trailer will damage it. If possible keep the heavy stuff in the car and the sails and clothing in the boat. The type of trailer is important too, and the wider the area over which the hull is supported the better.

The worst type are those that balance the boat on three or four tiny rubber pads. Better are the type with moulded fibreglass supports that are shaped to fit right round the hull. But these need to fit well to work properly. Gunwale-hung trailers have been popular for a while, although some designs do need the gunwales reinforced to be strong enough. The combination of gunwale supports with a soft

a) trolley with pads.

b) moulded fibreglass supports.

c) moulded fibreglass supports.

d) gunwhale hung. (*Mark Chisnell*)

strop that takes up the shape of the boat is one of the best alternatives. Even better is the Continental style which uses a mesh of straps to support the whole of the hull.

The trailer's suspension is also a consideration. One of the reasons that roof-racking is popular amongst dinghy sailors is that cars have considerably better suspension than trailers. The boat will get a much smoother and less damaging ride on the top of your car than bouncing along behind it. If you do roof-top the boat you will not need to be so worried about the way the hull is supported. And with many classes the boat can rest comfortably upside down on its deck and so protect the hull completely. The other advantage of this system, assuming that the car is big enough to do it safely, is that you are not restricted to trailing speed limits and you will pay a lot less for ferry tickets without the trailer. The downside is that you need help to get it on and off the car roof.

However you shift the boat around, if you are using the roads you should consider a cover for the hull, to protect it from road dirt and chips. This is more a problem for trailed dinghies, where the hull is right down at road level, than keelboats and car toppers, where the hull is up high. It sounds obvious, but make sure everything is tied down properly. Stories are told, urban myth though they may be, of helmsmen arriving at regattas with an empty trailer, while the boat idles its time away in a hedgerow some-where. What is more likely is that something will get just loose enough to bump or chafe, digging a hole in your perfect finish before you even get to the start line. Foils lying loose and unprotected in the boat are easily damaged. As is rigging, left on a mast that is not tied down properly. Ideally you should remove all the rigging from a mast every time you transport it. This stops halyards, shrouds and trapeze wires flapping around, fatiguing the metal and rubbing the anodising or paint off. In practice it's a lot of trouble to go to for a hundred-mile trip, but worth it for anything over five hundred miles. At the least you should tie the rigging tight against the mast; taping it down every few feet works well.

If the regatta is on another continent you may well find yourself packing the boat into a container for the trip. This is often organised by the class association and you may not have too much control over the way the boats are packed in. If you are involved, then do it as securely as you possibly can. As a rule containers are not handled carefully, as evidenced by the number of them drifting around the oceans, and your boat will need to be tightly tied in with plenty of padding to get there safely. While it is on the ship it may well be sitting in a salty, humid environment and it is important to wash it thoroughly with fresh water and then let it dry before it is packed. Any salt water left on the boat will increase the chances of corrosion of fittings in transit. Stripping hull and mast of fittings and then packing everything inside separate covers or watertight containers is the best solution if you have the time.

The final means of transporting the boat to the venue is to sail it there. Advice on such a trip is probably better left to the dozens of books on cruising. In addition you should think about limiting the damage, or the potential for damage, to your racing gear. Use some old sails, and keep the boat under-powered so you do not load everything up fully, especially short-handed when it is breezy. If the boat is at sea for a day or two, think about cleaning the bottom when you get there, hiring a diver or getting it lifted out so that you can hit it once with some fine, wet sandpaper. Try and avoid doing the trip in bad weather, as throwing the boat around in a gale can only shorten its racing life.

At the Venue

Ensuring the boat's reliability and limiting the potential for damaging gear failure does not stop when you arrive at the event. However you get there, when you arrive you should rig the boat carefully, checking everything again as you do it. The number of people who arrive at the venue and rig the boat leaving the spinnaker halyard at the top of the mast or forgetting to put the burgee in never ceases to amaze. If you miss such obvious things you are not going to notice the nut on the spreader retaining bolt that dropped out with the vibration en route, until its absence pops the spreader out backwards and takes the mast with it the first time you go sailing. Wash off any road or travel dirt as you put the boat together. Keeping the grit out of fittings and ropes lengthens their life.

You should have a list of items to check each day, which will be a smaller version of the full, pre-event check. Of course even that is not necessarily enough. There is a story about Tornado gold medallists Reg White and John Osborne, who had a pre-race checklist with over eighty items. The one that broke, Osborne's trapeze harness hook, wasn't on the list. Nevertheless, it is no bad idea to have some kind of formal system for checking the boat before you go afloat. Just looking at it carefully might enable you to pick up something that you would otherwise have missed.

Spares and Tools

However well prepared your boat is, at some stage gear failure will strike; the margins with which racing boats are built and rigged make it inevitable. So what spares and tools should you take with you to cover for this eventuality?

This will depend to a great extent on where the regatta is and how you travel there. Some venues have excellent local chandlers with good levels of modern equipment stock, but many do not. Phoning the club holding the event, or asking someone you know who has sailed there before, may help you decide what you should take. And of course there are all those things that may be unique to your particular boat. You will probably not find a two- or three-metre-long International 14 tiller extension in a sleepy seaside chandler used to just the local keelboat one-designs.

If you are driving and towing your boat to the event then there should be no problem in carrying everything you think you need. It is only when the boat is shipped abroad and you fly to meet it, or you double-trail the boat with someone else, that space becomes an issue – what to take and what to leave behind? In that case priority should always be given to the specialist items not readily available – spars and foils are the best examples. You should also look at sharing spares with someone else who is going. You would be particularly unfortunate for one mast, rudder and centreboard not to be sufficient between two of you, for instance. The other limiting factor is money. What spares can you afford to buy? Again, having those specialist items such as spars and foils is much more important than carrying around several hundred pounds worth of blocks and jammers.

When it comes to tools I am firmly of the opinion that the more you can afford to buy and carry around with you the better. We all know a boat park scrounger, the type who turns up without so much as a penknife to maintain his boat, and spends most of the regatta wandering around the boat park or marina trying to borrow a screwdriver or drill. Keeping this stuff organised, both tools and spares, is just about as important as having it. Again we all know the character whose car boot looks like the odds and sods bin in your local chandlery – full, but with little that is useful, and what is, is buried so deep you could not find it anyway. Buying a good tool box and splitting up your spares into separate containers for blocks, pulleys, shackles and so on may not seem like a crucial regatta winning move . . . But consider the two-race day when you have already lost the first race due to gear failure and you are struggling to get the boat fixed and back out on the water for the second start. Not being able to find x, y or z widget, which you are sure you have got, could lose you the race both practically and mentally.

A further consideration is what to carry with you on the water in the way of spares and tools. Even for the smallest dinghy this ought to include at least a shackle key, knife and a few spare lengths of line and shackles. Keelboats and small yachts can afford something more comprehensive, perhaps a couple of screwdrivers, spanners, a hacksaw and a pair of vice grips, along with some more shackles and blocks and perhaps some fastenings. This kit should be maintained with the same care as everything else. You do not want to carry the weight of vice grips around in the boat for a season only to find they have rusted solid by the time you actually need them. You can also vary the size of your toolkit and spares with the conditions; for a light airs race you may decide to carry nothing, and load it back on the next time there is breeze.

The availability of a coach boat can make a big difference, since they can carry everything that you might need before or between races. But make sure you have some system for finding your coach in an emergency. At a big event with a hundred or so boats, finding one rubber boat among many may not be easy, especially if they are supporting more than one crew. The obvious additional items to put in a coach boat are spinnaker poles (all too easily thrown overboard by excitable forward hands), spare or alternate sails, trapeze harnesses and perhaps even a boom if it is breezy. Along with a full toolkit and a better selection of blocks, shackles, jammers and ropes. If this level of preparation does not keep you in the series, you can blame bad luck with a clean conscience.

Chapter 5

Boat Systems

We have looked in some detail at how the boat will arrive at the regatta venue in one piece, and stay that way through a tough championship. This is the minimum requirement for your boat preparation. The next question is whether or not it works efficiently, and finally whether or not it goes fast – which we will look at in the next chapter. So do all the ropes do what they are supposed to, and are they the right kind of systems for the racing you will be doing? This is a topic that could be covered in great detail (*Dinghy Systems* by Chisnell and Hodgart, Waterline Books) but here we will restrict the discussion to some general points directly relevant to regatta preparation.

Systems to Suit

Even a cursory glance across a dinghy park (unless it is filled with a particularly strict one-design) will convince you that there are many different ways to rig a racing yacht. When you set up a boat with a view to winning a championship regatta, personal preference is high on the list of priorities. And not just for you as helmsman, owner or skipper, but for the crew as well. It is difficult, however, to know what you do or do not like about a particular set of systems on a boat without sailing one for a reasonable period of time. When I am moving into a new class I prefer to buy a good second-hand boat and see how others have solved the particular problems presented by that class before trying to do so myself. You often find that what seemed awkward or inconvenient when you looked at it in the dinghy park for the first time, in fact turns out to be a good idea after a few weeks' sailing.

The first time I sailed a Tornado was a good lesson in this approach. Invited to crew at the 1990 World Championships I first stepped on to the boat a couple of days before the practice race (which may sound like one for the book on how not to prepare for a regatta, except that the event I had in mind was two years away and in Barcelona). I couldn't get on with the trapeze system as it was and spent the rest of the day altering it to the systems more usually seen on high-performance monohulls. By the end of the week I had changed it all back again after acknowledging that there were several perfectly good reasons why it had been like that in the first place. In contrast, I have a complete inability to remember to pull a traveller to windward after I tack, and this is something that I always avoid when I am helming. So when I arrived at a 470 World Championship and picked up a charter boat that had a traveller, it came straight off and stayed off. Personal preference is important, but until you have experience in the class or with the system, temper it heavily with what other people are using.

Your crew's opinions are also an important consideration. You should allow them, as far as possible, a free run at their end of the boat. There is no point forcing spinnaker bags on a crew that has never used them and has no wish to do so now. I would, however, insist that they sail with something for a while before changing it, unless they have a lot of experience with the class. You must also address where the overlaps are, which controls are run to which people. Dividing responsibilities is something we have already discussed and you should think about the impact it has on how the boat is laid out. If your crewman is also your sailmaker then he may well be better off with the sail controls. If you have brought him along to do the tactics, let him keep his head out of the boat while you pull the strings.

Horses for Courses

As you look forward to the main event of the season you should consider the type of venue and courses that will be used. As this is written, sailing is going through tremendous changes with regard to the format of the racing. Championship events may no longer be decided on the traditional, triangular course with one- or two-mile beats and a couple of laps. And you may find yourself on a race course with shorter legs and more corners, which puts a premium on boathandling rather than boat speed.

If this is the case you might need to rethink your boat layout, if it has been set up with the more traditional courses in mind. Simplicity and ease of use are at a premium on short courses, whereas adjustability, to refine the final ounce of speed out of the rig, is more important on long legs. The cunningham and outhaul, for instance, can be left on the mast and boom rather than run all the way back to the helmsman, since you will not have time to adjust them anyway. Spinnaker chutes may find a renaissance because they have always advantaged boathandling rather than speed. Complicated and infinitely variable rig set-ups may be better replaced by lighter and more reliable chainplates. Hoops and travellers could be replaced by simple strops, or aft sheeting. Even major decisions such as rig type may be affected by course orientation. Bendy rigs usually adjust to conditions more easily than straight rigs, which necessarily rely on raking, and subsequent tweaking of the rest of the settings, to depower.

You should also consider the likely conditions of wind and water. This is something we will look at when we come to the chapters on boat speed and weather preparation. The conditions have a more general relevance to the boat's layout and efficiency. If you spend much of the early part of the season in club or local regattas, perhaps on inland waters and in light airs, you may get away with equipment deficiencies that become glaringly obvious when you get to the season's big regatta with waves and a lot of breeze. Worse still, you may be convinced to change to systems ultimately inappropriate to other conditions. It is important to consider how well everything will work under conditions of maximum stress and difficulty, rather than how it all copes with a relaxed, sunny club race. How are you going to feel about that spinnaker pole uphaul block that catches occasionally, but is easy to free, when the crew has to go forward to clear it in ten-foot waves and twenty-five knots? Your spinnaker downhaul rope may lead perfectly to a standing position, but what about when you have to drop it on a windy reach – flat-out hiking? Only by doing a lot of sailing in different conditions and on different courses can you be confident that your boat is ready for anything. This is why it is so dangerous to take a new boat to a championship. New boats are fine, but allow time to work them up when you plan your campaign.

Efficiency

Whatever systems you finally decide to use on your boat, the over-riding factor that should be considered is whether or not they work. By working we mean do they achieve the intended objective, and do they physically work. A mainsheet system can apparently work, all the pulleys run, it goes in and out, but if you cannot get the necessary sail shape it is not achieving the objective. So by the time you get to the regatta, not only should all the friction have been removed from the systems and everything that can catch or snag been eradicated, but also the rig tension systems should be capable of getting the tension you require, the jib leads should run right through the range of positions that the jib will need, the vang should have the purchase for you to be able to pull it on tight in thirty knots, but also allow the boom up enough in light airs downwind, and so on.

Rules

Many classes are subject to rules that will form part of the regatta sailing instructions: class rules, measurement rules and perhaps safety regulations for offshore sailors. It is important to acquire a copy of the Notice of Race early in the season to discover exactly what conditions you will be sailing under. We will look at the Notice of Race in more detail in Chapter 9. For dinghies it is normally straightforward enough, the class rules suffice. But beware of recent rule interpretations, particularly in international or Olympic classes where constant pressure on the rule will bring constant adjustment by committees. There is nothing worse than having to rip off your brand new go-faster widget that you copied from a boat you saw at the last regatta because it has since been ruled illegal.

For bigger boats there can be a quite awesome plethora of rules, including local regulations, sometimes regarding safety, to comply with. Thoroughly checking everything is the only way to be sure there are no nasty surprises in store. Black bands are a classic example. The number of people who hook up their mainsail to the same place every time they go sailing – without realising they have pulled it over the black band – is quite astounding. If the only time it is checked by officialdom is after you have got a gun at a major championship, it is too late.

Whatever boat you sail you cannot check its rule compliance carefully enough. Almost all major regattas now include some form of either pre- or post-race measurement checking and you cannot afford to lose a good result because your boat did not comply. The more important the event, the more intense this measurement frenzy will become. The competitors will start to join in, analysing other boats and putting in protests that are disruptive and distracting even when they fail. In the 470 class I have seen people waste an afternoon chipping non-slip tape off the gunwales, when they could have been sailing, because they infringed a rule that had been abused for so long everyone had forgotten about it – except the committee at this particular event. Many people feel the New Zealanders lost the Challenger's slot for the 1992 *America*'s Cup because they were hopelessly distracted by *Il Moro*'s measurement protest over their use of the bowsprit. When they lost the protest, they lost the event. The lesson is to make sure your boat is whiter than white. Any hassle over boat measurement will detract from your chances of winning, and it may even cost you the regatta.

Chapter 6
Boat Speed

Good boat speed is fundamental to your chances of winning a championship regatta. A full examination of what makes sailboats fast or slow would take up this whole book and probably a couple more like it. What I do want to cover here is how to approach the problem in relation to your regatta programme, so the first thing is to recommend some good background reading. Lawrie Smith's trilogy – *Tuning Your Dinghy*, *Tuning Yachts and Small Keelboats* and *Sailpower* (all with Fernhurst) – presents as clear an approach to the topic as you will find. I would also recommend Tom Whidden's *The Art and Science of Sails* as a definitive analysis of the motive force of yachts.

Once armed with a general background knowledge of boat tuning, how do you go about ensuring that you have good speed when you get to the event? And that is the first point: you must have your speed sorted before you arrive. Realising you are slow after you have arrived at the regatta, either in the preparatory period or in the first race, is usually a fatal blow to your prospects, as much because of the distraction it will provide from the other aspects of your racing as through the deficit in speed on the race course. So you must work on speed and be confident that you have it, prior to the regatta. But we are getting ahead of ourselves; first you will need to select some equipment. In the case of a strict one design class this may not seem like a particularly onerous task. But beware, even boats as simple as a Laser have their individual foibles, and with something like a 470 or International 14, choosing the gear is a major research project.

Equipment Choice

Unless you are a professional, be it sailmaker, spar or boatbuilder, or have been sailing your class for a long time, I feel strongly that there is only one way to approach the boat speed issue, and that is to copy what is already going quickly. It is rare these days that credible, major championships are won with breakthrough boat speed. When they are, that speed almost invariably belongs to someone in the marine industry who can (almost) justify on a commercial basis the phenomenal research investment. It is unlikely, if you have to hold down a job in the real world, sailing at weekends and maybe three or four weeks a year, that you are going to achieve championship winning speed from first principles. The only exception might be if you have been sailing the same class for five, or more likely ten years and have been researching boat speed for all that time. Otherwise the effort is much better expended on other areas of your sailing.

The best approach to getting boat speed is to buy the right kit with a comprehensive set of tuning instructions. Then devote your time to learning to use it effectively. It may sound harsh, but researching 470 sail shapes with your local sailmaker is not a cost-effective or efficient approach to winning. The same goes for any other highly competitive class, particularly International or Olympic classes, or those that have been around for a while. In all these cases the basic research will have been done and the sail shapes and set-ups figured out. It is your job to find something that suits your sailing style and then learn to use that as effectively as possible.

Remember, particularly if you do not already have the boat, that you are buying the whole package of hull, foils, sails and spar. The sails and spar are the two that must match, but the careful selection of hull and foils is just as important. If you have sailed in the class for a while then you will already have some idea of the options. If not, you will need to do some research. You are trying to discover what gear is common in the class, which is successful and how it is set up and used. Start by spending some time talking to sailors in the class; go to a couple of regattas and see what is winning. Once you have an idea of the two or three most common sail and spar combinations, hulls and foils, try and speak to the most successful users of this equipment. Ask them why they chose it and how they set it up. Have a good look at their boats, perhaps make a few notes and take some pictures. By now you should have a clear concept of each option: how the boat should be set up; whether it is with a deck or keel-stepped mast; used with a straight, raked rig or one that is allowed to bend; reputedly quicker in light air than in a breeze, flat water than a chop and so on. The more you can discover at this stage the more informed a choice you will be able to make later on.

Next, you must start to talk to the suppliers and begin by asking them the same questions. What was the thinking behind the design and how should you set up the equipment? Obviously in the case of hull and foils there is a limited amount they can tell you. But in the case of the sailmaker you want as much detail as you can get, most obviously which mast section the sail was designed for,

and all the set-up numbers. Don't be put off with general-
ities or waffle. What you want are specific numbers and
instructions on how the gear is supposed to be set up in
different conditions: mast rake and spreader settings,
chocking or deck control, jib lead positions, and so on. All
the time think about whether what you are hearing ties in
with what the sailors have already told you. It certainly
will if the sailmaker is also the top sailor in the class –
which is not uncommon. Be wary of getting a suit of sails
which are only being used successfully by the loft's star
jockey; the chances are he is the reason for the boat speed,
not the sails. If it all makes sense you are on the right
track; if not, or if you cannot get the information, look
somewhere else, because what you are buying is just the
sails – what you should be buying is the boat speed.

After all this talking you will finally have to make a
decision: what gear are you going to buy? This may be easy
and it may be hard, depending on the results of your
research. There may be a clear market leader whose kit is
quick and can provide you with all the information you
need to get the boat going. But if there is no clear con-
tender you will have to consider other factors. The priority is if one rig type seems more suited to your campaign.
Perhaps it has an emphasis on simplicity and flexibility
through the wind range and you are the type of sailor who
hates fiddling with controls – this rig was made for you.
Maybe it is a heavyweight's rig and you are at the top of
the competitive weight range. Maybe, and this is more
risky, it is a light air rig and your big regatta is a light air
venue.

Personally, I have never been in favour of one condition
sails, particularly for one-designs where there is usually a
sail limitation. Be especially careful of buying these
unknowingly – last year's championship might have been

won in a week of strong breezes at a venue famous for them, with a set of sails designed for that purpose. If this year's championship is anywhere else you will need a more all-round suit, so find some that are winning across a range of conditions and go for those. We have all heard the phrase, 'it's not normally like this here', so be careful if you decide to go for anything other than an all-round suit. There is nothing worse than knowing you have a heavy-weather suit of sails in a light air regatta.

If nothing still marks one option out from the rest you come down to such staple consumer variables as price, quality and service. You should always look for a good deal, but if one product is clearly the best you can expect to have to pay for it. Quality of finish is important: you want the sails to last and cloth weight comes into this equation as well. Some sails may have a reputation for being fast out of the box but only lasting for one regatta. Service comes down to your relationship with the individual company, how important your custom is, whether you get on with them, how efficient they are, and so on. It also helps if they are based nearby, as getting repairs done and picking up new sails to tight deadlines becomes easier. Building a relationship with someone will help ensure that you get looked after, so sticking with the same people does have advantages, but I think it is low on the list of decisive factors. Remember – what you are buying first and foremost is performance on the water.

You may have some or all of your equipment for next season, in which case your research should be targeted at how best to set it up. I have included below the type of tuning guide that you are looking for.

Now it is up to you to set the boat up according to the numbers. You will need to know how to measure the mast

hyde

hyde sails

Hyde Sails Limited,
263 Church Road, Benfleet,
Essex SS7 4QR, England.
Tel: 0268 756254
Fax: 0268 565075

470 Tuning Guide

Proctor Epsilon,
Code 2M Mainsail Code 2I jib and Code 2J Spinnaker,
Sails as supplied to I.Y.R.U. Worlds,

The measurements and dimensions that are listed here are intended as a guide when initially setting up your rig. As you become more familiar with the Hyde rig, you will gather your own information and data of how you should adjust the rig to suit your particular style of sailing and the infinite number of conditions you will encounter.

Spreader Length		475mm	
	Mast Rake	**Spreader Deflection**	**Rig Tension**
1. Non Trapezing	22'2''	5 1/2''	36
	675cm	14cm	
2. High Trapezing	22'	4 3/8''	36
	670cm	11.2cm	
3. Full Trapezing	21'11''	4 3/8''	36
	668cm	11.2cm	
4. Overpowered	21'9''	4 3/8''	36
	663cm	11.2cm	
5. Very Overpowered			
	21'7''	4' 3/4''	36
	658cm	12.5cm	

Hyde Sails Limited
Reg. in England No. 1530833
Vat No. 368 7828 88

I Y R U
OFFICIAL
SUPPLIER TO
THE 1994 IYRU
WORLD SAILING
CHAMPIONSHIP

The first page of the 470 tuning guide for Hyde Sails Epsilon Rig, reproduced with permission from Hyde Sails Ltd.

rake, spreader deflection and length and rig tension (which is included later on in the guide). After that it is a day in the dinghy park setting it all up. Then it comes down to familiarity. Boat speed is as much a function of your ability to set up the equipment as it is of the equipment itself. And it will only go quickly across the wind range when you are completely comfortable with where everything sets up in different conditions. This is where your on-the-water boat tuning efforts should be directed. Rather than testing different equipment, you should be testing the small detail of the set-up, comfortable in the knowledge that your gear is capable of championship-winning performance.

Changing Gears

We can take the 470 as an example. It is a boat where speed is determined to a great extent by the mast rake which, in turn, is decided to a similar extent before the start. In the 470 the shrouds are on pinned chainplates and so are effectively locked off from the five-minute gun. You can adjust the jib halyard, but as you increase the rake by easing the halyard you also progressively lose the rig tension. As a consequence the headstay sags, which powers up the jib – a problem when raking to depower.

The tuning sheet you will get from most manufacturers gives several settings of rake, tension, spreaders and mast bend – like the one in the illustration. So you twiddle around in the dinghy park until you know where to set the halyard and shrouds and spreaders to achieve these settings and then off you go sailing. This works for a while, until the first time that you get caught in a race where the conditions have radically altered. You start in five knots and end up sailing in twenty-five for instance.

I have memories of a particularly painful experience of this at a 470 regatta in Playa d'Aro. We dropped the rig back but to no avail, it just didn't seem to help. After dragging in at the back half of the fleet with the main flogging and the boat hopelessly unbalanced it was clear that we were doing something wrong. The leaders had somehow managed to adjust everything to keep the boat balanced; mains were full and driving, the boat flat and fast. We talked to some of the guys who had been up the front at the end and deduced that we needed different ways of setting up for each rake that we used: one that was a little softer on the rig tension and so would allow us to pull it upright if the wind went down, and one that was a little tighter than normal so allowing us to drop it back if the wind went up. Before the race we would make a judgement on whether the breeze was likely to go up or down and use the setting that would correspond to this eventuality. So if it was blowing ten knots and threatening to increase we would use the 8-12 knot rake, but on a tighter than normal forestay. This gave us the scope to ease the halyard as the breeze increased, giving us more rake but with a forestay tension still close to normal. We got out the tape measure and the rig tension gauge and spent a day getting the various permutations right, and recording them on a settings sheet that was an idiot's guide to boat tune.

This is the sort of lesson that you must learn in your preparation time prior to the regatta. Once you have the basic set-up you must get out on the water and test your speed. This is done through a combination of tuning runs and regatta sailing. The lesson above was only learned through regatta conditions – if we had been out there tuning we would probably have stopped the test and reset the shrouds before we had a chance to realise that other people were dealing with the situation better than we

Wind	Up or Down	Pin	Halyard Hook	Tension	Rake	Prebend	Chock
0-4	-	3b	1	35.5	22' 2"	48mm	0
6-8	-	3b	1	35.5	22' 2"	48mm	5
8-12	up	3f	1 then 2.5	35.5 then 32	22' 2" then 22' 0.5"	48 then 50mm	15
12-18	up	2b	2 then 3.5	36 then 32	21' 11.5" then 21' 9"	72 then 69mm	0
18+	up	2f	2.5 then 3.8	36 then 32.5	21' 10" then 21' 8.5"	75 then 73mm	0
18+	down	2b	3.25 then 1.75	33 then 36	21' 10" then 22' 0.25"	63 then 61mm	0
12-18	down	3f	2.5 then 1.5	33 then 36	21' 11.5" then 22' 1"	60mm	0

Tuning sheet that might be developed from the original guide, modified and detailed for a specific boat and crew.

were. Nevertheless, tuning runs are a crucial part of your boat speed search. And the one thing you will need for these is a tuning partner.

The ideal partner is someone about your standard, perhaps a little better, with similar ambitions and resources. It is great if you can agree on a programme for the whole season, but linking up with someone for just one regatta or training session will do. The most important aspects of the relationship are trust and honesty, and the belief that you will both gain the most from sticking to these principles. The type of people you want to avoid are the ones who will use tuning sessions to score mental points against you.

Once you have found your tuning partner, you need to agree a programme. If you are both targeting the same championship through a season's preparation then you have the perfect arrangement. Perhaps you can organise some weekends of training together, or you both agree to arrive at other regatta venues a few days early. You need to plan your sessions before you go on the water so that you know what you are trying to achieve when you get out there and can get straight on with it. What you should be aiming for is finding the fastest settings for your equipment across the range of conditions. This involves sailing beside your tuning partner for mile after mile, upwind and down. Progress will only come through a methodical approach, refining things slowly, one at a time, and taking plenty of notes so that you can always back-track.

I have seen so many tuning runs develop into chaos that it seems worthwhile going over some do's and don'ts. Always remember the objective is not to beat the other boat, but to learn. Set the tuning run up so that both boats are even at the beginning, on the same tack with clear air and the same speed. They should be close enough to be sailing in the same wind and water, but without affecting each other. In practice this is about three or four boat lengths apart. Don't try and get an edge that you have not earned, jumping the gun, sheeting in early and ruining the test. Also don't deliberately sail the boat to take the other guy's air. Try to pull ahead and sail faster for sure, but don't deliberately give up a windward advantage to sail over the other boat. Keep your height and try to go forwards on him instead.

You might agree to sail for ten or fifteen minutes on each run, or until someone has a clear edge. Once you have agreed who is quicker, you should confirm that the edge is not because of a wind shift. A header will make the leeward boat look good and a lift will do the same for the windward boat. Then swap places, the leeward boat going to windward and vice versa, and run the test again without changing anything else. If you get the same result, give the slower boat the opportunity to change something, and keep the faster boat the same. If your co-operation extends this far, compare the set-ups before you do this, especially if you have the same equipment.

Once you have decided on the change, start another tuning run and see if it has helped the slower boat. If not, change something else and keep doing it until the slower boat is quicker. Then give the new, slower boat the opportunity to change something. In this way you should be able to leapfrog the pace of both boats forwards. Talking and comparing notes on the changes you have made will make the process even quicker for both of you. Some partners may not wish to help to this extent, but if they are willing it will speed up the whole business.

You can see now where the honesty and trust come in. It is so easy to sabotage these tuning affairs without the other person knowing. You can sail the boat a little more

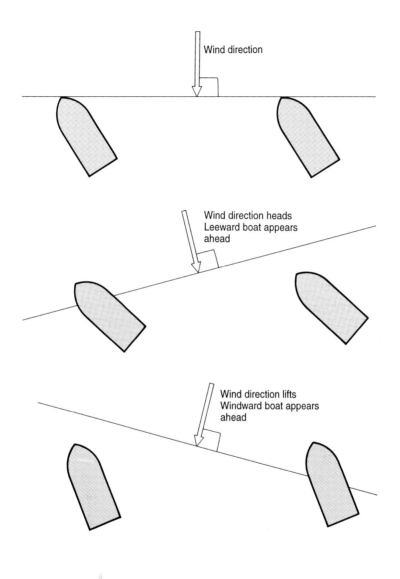

The effect of windshifts on boat tuning runs.

slowly, to make them think they have improved when they have not, lie about the changes you have made that are making you go quicker or slower and so on. If done subtly it would be impossible for the victim to detect what was happening. And he would not just be wasting his time, but actually going backwards in his knowledge. So you have to do this with someone you can trust. But when it is done properly a season's work with a good tuning partner, combined with careful selection of the right equipment, will ensure that you go into the final regatta with the best possible potential speed.

Technique

Finally we should consider the other 'forgotten' element of boat speed – sailing technique. It is rarely a part of the technical speed discussions you hear in marinas, dinghy parks and club bars, but it is at least as important. Buying the right equipment and setting it up the right way is only part of the story. It is how you sail the boat that counts in the end. In classes that are becoming increasingly refined and standardised in equipment, the difference comes down more and more to technique.

The best way to improve your technique is out there on the water. It is by sailing that you will learn how the boat prefers to be sailed in the myriad conditions that you might meet on a championship race-course; light winds and big left over waves, flat water and a gale, short chop, a long swell, gusty conditions and so on. And for much of this work you do not need a tuning partner, you can and should develop a feel for when the boat is fast by sailing on your own.

Obviously how you set the boat up, with balance and sail shape, is a part of your technique, and a tuning partner will help to clarify results. But think about how you are actually sailing the boat too, and how it feels when you make changes. Is it better to point than free off in some conditions compared to others? How does your crew move his body over waves when he is trapezing or hiking? What is the precise best moment to pump when surfing downwind? Do you know the optimum angles to sail in all conditions? How smoothly do you work together? Do you find that sometimes your crew has moved inboard while you have eased the mainsheet? Do you work against each other to balance the boat as much as you work together?

Nobody does all this stuff perfectly all the time. There are so many aspects to sailing the boat, that it is impossible to be perfect. And if it is impossible to sail the boat perfectly, you can always get better. So it is worth practising – it all converts directly into speed. And boat speed wins races, there is no substitute for it.

Part 3

Strategic Planning

Chapter 7
Geography at the Venue

As the competition gets tighter at the front of the toughest one-design fleets, the big regattas are becoming harder to win though the application of percentage sailing tactics. If you have a boat speed edge and there are only one or two people in the fleet who are fast enough to stay ahead of you through a two hour race, then you can afford to sail conservatively. Keeping close to your competitors and away from the corners. But when no one has a boat-speed edge, and any one of twenty boats that gets round the first mark ahead is quick enough to stay there, you have a different sort of problem. You have to be up there at the windward mark, and to achieve that you have to go the right way up the first beat – choose a side and commit to it proactively. Rather than just avoid going the wrong way, by reacting to what is going on around you as the leg progresses.

If we define strategy as the overall plan for the leg, and tactics as the minute by minute decisions you make in dealing with the situation around you, then strategy has become much more important in modern fleet racing conditions. You should be using tactics to make your strategy happen – but how do you figure out a strategy in the first place?

Good strategy comes down to good preparation. All the

elements should be in place days or even weeks before the big event. This and the next chapter are all about where you go to look for the right information. First we will deal with researching the physical geography of the venue. This will affect the race-course in two ways; by the motion of the water through tide or current, and secondly by the effect the local landscape will have on the wind. If this kind of strategic thinking is new to you and you are wondering what you are supposed to do with the information we are about to find, then there is some reading you should do first.

On the topic of tides and currents have a look at David Arnold's *Tides and Currents*, published by Fernhurst books. To understand the effect of the landscape on the wind David Houghton's books are essential, *Wind Strategy* and *Weather at Sea*, again both published by Fernhurst. These books also provide an essential background to meteorology that you will need when assessing the weather forecasts we will be looking at in the next chapter. David has developed a theory of sea breezes that seems to have been widely accepted by sailing forecasters and racers worldwide, and these books provide an essential introduction to it. Considering the number of regattas that are held on hot coastlines subject to sea breeze effects, it is a topic you cannot afford to ignore. Once you have digested all that, you should look at Jean-Yves Bernot's 'Tips from the Top' book from Waterline, *Bernot on Breezes*, which carries David's theories a little further with some French research. Other sources on developing strategies are books on tactics. I have always thought that this is a difficult subject to write about, because sailing tactics are such a complex affair, with so many possible variations. Probably the most rigorous attempts in the field are by the American, Stuart Walker. Personally, I have always found his explanations a little too dry and academic to be gripping, but if you can cope with them they are probably the most rigorous analysis of sailboat tactics that you will find. Try *Advanced Racing Tactics* from Angus and Robertson, or *Positioning: the Logic of Sailboat Racing* published by W W Norton. My own favourites on tactics are Dave Perry's *Winning in One-Designs*, published by Adlard Coles, which is a general analysis of the title's topic, but has the tactical chapters as the high point. There is also the excellent *Championship Tactics* by Tom Whidden, Gary Jobson and Adam Loory and published by Nautical Books, which is a much wider review of the topic than Perry provides with more material applicable to keelboats and yachts – both are excellent books.

Before You Leave

Once you have a grip of sailboat tactics your next problem (apart from learning to apply them properly!) is to research the information that you need. Where you find it will depend on which country you are sailing in, and which country you are researching the material from. As a general rule the best place to start is your local chandlery or bookshop. You will need one that has a yacht clientele rather than dinghy customers, because they will stock charts and pilot books, which is what you are looking for. If you live a hundred miles from the ocean and there is nothing suitable nearby, check out the sailing magazines for mail order bookshops, phone them up and tell them what you want, or get a catalogue. If you are racing in the British Isles, then you will be spoilt for such information, with the many excellent Admiralty charts and associated publications. But most other countries that are developed enough to be running sailboat races will have similar material.

The first thing you are after is a chart of the venue, and this is the case regardless of what type of racing you are doing – day racing or offshore, in dinghies or yachts. You should be able to get a chart through the bookshop as we have discussed above. If they do not stock them they should be able to pass you on to someone who does, perhaps the hydrographic office or publisher responsible for producing them. Many of these people publish charts for around the world, not just the home or national waters. A good example is the British Admiralty: wherever you are racing in the world they will probably have a chart for it. If local searches have failed to turn anything up, then you can get Admiralty charts mail order from one of their Class A Admiralty Chart Agents. To find the one closest, you can phone the Hydrographic Office on +44 (0)1823 337 900. They can tell you the nearest chart agent, wherever you are in the world.

You should get hold of the largest scale chart you can find for the area. This will tell you a lot. It will give you a feel for the immediate geography of the region, whether the coastline is rocky and high or flat and muddy. Combining this with the weather research we will discuss in the next chapter and the ideas in the books mentioned above, it will allow you to assess how the shoreline will affect the wind. It will also allow you to see the water you will be sailing on. How deep is it? Does it look like it will be vulnerable to long swells or a short chop? Which wind directions blow unheeded on to the course and which will be travelling over nearby land? We will look at how some of these things may affect other aspects of your preparation in the next chapter.

The other topic that is crucial to your research into the

physical geography of the area is tidal or current flow. Your first clues to this will come from the chart – are there any tidal diamonds? On Admiralty charts these are signified by a diamond shape with a letter in the middle. The letter refers you to a table of tidal flow rate and direction that will be found somewhere else on the chart. To use this you will need to find a tide table for the reference port. Again the Admiralty do produce books of these, but you may be better off with a local pilot book or almanac – we will come on to these in a moment. Once you know the high water time you can calculate which way the water will be flowing and how fast at any time and date, crucial information for good tactics.

Your chart may not have any tidal diamonds, but even if it does it is only a start. You need more detailed information if you can find it, preferably tidal atlases which show you how fast and where the water will be flowing on miniature charts for every hour or even half hour of the tide state. These are used in a similar way to the tidal diamond. They will be based round high water at a reference port. You will need a tide table for that reference port so you can look up the high water time for the days you will be racing. Once you know that, it is straightforward to work through the tidal atlas, marking up each page with the correct time of the day at which that particular tidal state occurs. Then, come race day, you just flick through the pages to get a complete picture of the changing tidal situation.

For some places tidal atlases are easy to find; the English Solent, for instance, is well covered, as is Long Island Sound on the east coast of the United States. Other places will not be so easy to find information on. Again, you should start at the bookshop; you may find what you are looking for in a specific tidal atlas for the area. Several

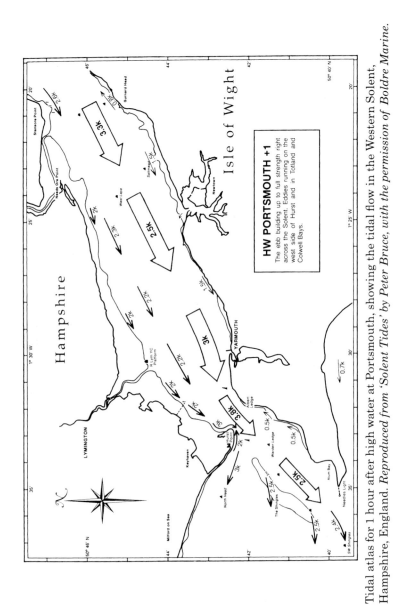

Tidal atlas for 1 hour after high water at Portsmouth, showing the tidal flow in the Western Solent, Hampshire, England. *Reproduced from 'Solent Tides' by Peter Bruce, with the permission of Boldre Marine.*

publishers produce a series of these and one of them may cover the area that you are looking at.

The other alternatives are pilot books or almanacs. These collect all the valuable information for one particular area in a single volume and are produced by a variety of nautical publishers. They are generally orientated towards our cruising brethren, but often you can find valuable local information in the pages. This might well include those sought-after tidal stream atlases, but also descriptions of local weather patterns. We will look at this aspect in more detail in the next chapter. It may well be difficult to access this information if you live a long way from the venue you are researching. It is hard to justify buying a couple of almanacs mail order when you are unsure of how useful they are going to be. So it may pay to wait until you can wander round the local chandleries at the venue. This is always one of my first tasks when I arrive in a new area.

Of course, if after all this effort you have still been unsuccessful, it is possible that the reason you cannot find a tidal atlas is that there is either no tide or no one has ever got around to measuring it at this venue. In which case you must wait until you arrive locally to do your research, and then it must be done on the water. Whether you have compiled a stack of information or only managed to find a chart of the race-course, the routine is much the same once you reach the regatta venue. In the first instance you will be checking the theories and ideas that you have developed, in the other you will be building them from first principles.

At the Venue

This is why it is so important to be at the venue early, with all the rest of your preparation completed. You do not want to be sitting on the dock rebuilding your boat while others are out there checking the wind bends and the tidal streams. The most important aspect of this stage of your preparation is careful observation of weather and current. Weather we will come on to in a moment; current checking should be a systematic part of every day you spend on the water prior to the start of your regatta.

Tide Sticks and Measurements

The easiest way to observe the current flow is to look at any marks or buoys fixed to the seabed; you should be able to see how the water is flowing around them. It is unusual to find a venue without any navigation marks near the course, or at least the occasional crab or lobster pot. With a little practice you will be able to assess visually the current strength, but to begin with you may need a tide stick to help you. A tide stick is a pole with flotation at one end, such as a sealed plastic bottle, and weight at the other, perhaps a lump of lead or just a brick or stone. The weight keeps it sitting vertically in the water and the flotation keeps it just afloat, illustration opposite.

It should then be carried along by the current or tide, unaffected by the wind. You will need a stopwatch to time its passage past the fixed mark using the length of the boat as a measure of distance. Remember that:

$$velocity = \frac{distance}{time.}$$

If you use the boat length in metres and time in seconds you will get a result in metres per second. So if the boat is four metres long and the stick travels two boat lengths in twelve seconds, then:

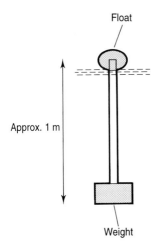

Float

Approx. 1 m

Weight

Tide stick.

$$\text{tidal velocity} = \frac{(4 \times 2)}{12} = 0.66 \text{ m/s}$$

To convert this number to knots, which is the measure of speed that most tide tables use, you must multiply the metres per second value by the conversion factor of 1.945:

So 0.66 m/s = 0.66 × 1.945 = 1.28 knots.

In fact doubling it will be more than accurate enough for our purposes! Once you know the speed you can use a hand bearing compass to sight the direction in which the tide is going and measure the bearing. Current is always measured in the direction to which it is flowing rather than where it is coming from. You should note down these results and compare them to whatever predictions you have been able to research. Make these measurements and comparisons at as many places on the race-course and at as many different times as you can. How do they match your predictions? Does the tide run consistently early or late? You should look for reasons to explain what you see. Is the wind affecting the tide, or rain in rivers swelling the ebb? If you can find reasonable explanations your observations will become much more useful later on. If the conditions remain the same it is reasonable to assume that the variations will remain the same. If they change you can expect the variations to disappear, perhaps to be replaced by others – what those are you have to figure out!

If you have no predictions then you will have to be a little more systematic in where and when you take your measurements, since you need to build up your own tidal atlas. Pick three or four marks near or on the race-course and try to check the tide on them at least every couple of hours through the day. This is where it is nice to have your own support boat, since you can get round your marks a lot quicker and more efficiently, and on a more regular basis, without the inconvenience of having to sail to them or break into your other sailing work. You should record your findings and try to see a pattern and explanations. Is it a conventional six-hour tidal flow or just a steady wind-blown current? Only careful research will tell you.

But even outside your systematic mark checking, always keep your eyes open for anything strange or unusual. Reference your line of sailing against the land whenever you can to see if you are starting to slide one way or the other on an unexpected current. Back eddies and tidelines develop and disappear at different states of the tide; finding them may give you an edge over the opposition you had not expected.

Local Knowledge

Finally we should consider the mythical pre-regatta project of talking to the locals. Personally I have never been much in favour of this. I have seen local folklore ('always go into the beach when it's in the west') turned on its head so many times that I don't have much faith in it. But if you can find someone who lives locally but is capable of national or international results then it is worth talking to them. The trouble is, if they are any good, the chances are someone will have lent them a boat and they will be racing against you! Whoever you talk to, always ask yourself, and them, why? Why go into the beach when it's in the west? Is there more wind in there? A shift? Tidal advantage? In which case, at what state of tide should you 'always' go into the beach when it is in the west? If you can get a satisfactory explanation, or better still get out there with your tuning partner and test the theory, then keep it in the back of your mind. If not, beware.

Chapter 8
The Weather

Historical Data

The second area of research essential to developing good race strategy is the weather, and in this chapter we will look in a little more detail at the potential sources of weather information. The first issue is whether or not it is worth sourcing any historical information prior to the regatta. Sometimes regatta organisers are generous enough to provide this kind of information when you enter. Documentation tells you the probabilities of various wind directions and strengths for the venue at the time of year you will be there. The question is what value you should place on this information.

It is certainly interesting to take it and compare it to your chart of the race area and see what kind of conditions this indicates. Does the wind most commonly blow off the land or onshore? You can look at some potential strategies with these wind directions, figure out which are converging and diverging shores, the effect of islands or headlands and so on (referring to the ideas in David Houghton's book). Having thought ahead through these potential scenarios you are much better equipped and more quickly able to orientate yourself when you arrive at the venue.

A more complex issue is when people talk about, and the statistics often support, 'heavy weather' or 'light weather' venue categories. You need to ask yourself to what degree you are going to take account of this with regard to the preparation of the rest of your campaign. Are you going to pick a particularly light crew, alter the sail shapes or boat set-up, and so on? As I have already mentioned in the chapter on boat speed, I am wary of this kind of thing. Statistics only point out the average conditions, those you are most likely to get. The crucial aspect is: how much more likely? It may blow from the west at between fifteen and twenty-five knots for forty per cent of the time, but it still leaves a sixty percent chance it will do something else. It is always more conservative to establish a good overall set-up that is fast across a range of conditions than to put yourself in a corner of the performance optimisation curve. Of course you may not be the conservative type, and regattas are won by specialists when their conditions turn up for a whole week.

Deciding on your approach to this problem is as much to do with your personal temperament as anything else. I'm the conservative type, you may not be. But there are places where the probability of a particular condition is so strong that even the ultra-conservative need to take note. I hesitate to state an example, because someone will have been there when it was different, but Lake Garda (where the marks are left permanently in place because the wind is so consistent) is one venue you can just about rely on to get strong breeze. So how do you find out whether your regatta venue is like this? A little pre-regatta meteorological research does not go amiss.

A good start is to find someone who has raced there previously, preferably someone good, whose opinion you respect. Not only will they be able to tell you what it was like when they were there, but they will have heard all the stories and rumours about what it is supposed to be like. If you get the feeling from this that you're in for a mixed bag of conditions it is probably not worth taking the project any further. However, they may indicate that there is a good chance of it being heavily biased towards one type of condition or another, in which case you may well want to do some more checking.

The first place to look is any almanacs or pilot books you have managed to find on the area; these have often got background meteorological information in them, even if they are biased towards the concerns of the cruising yachtsman. The second job is to contact your local meteorological centre. They may be able to point you in the direction of information available at a local library or university. Some of them, such as the Bracknell Weather Centre in England, will be able to prepare a report on some venues for you. This will cost money, but if you are serious about researching the conditions it is the best solution.

However, you should keep a couple of things in mind. Firstly you need to know exactly where the recordings were taken. The problem is whether or not the station is subject to the same local and thermal effects as the racecourse. There is a famous story about the initial venue reports for the Seoul Olympics, where weather data provided by the Koreans indicated a light air venue. But when the British team officials checked they discovered the weather station was tucked behind a hill that protected it from the prevailing wind – and Seoul turned out to be one of the windiest Olympic regattas ever held. Similarly, if the readings were all taken two or three miles offshore, then they will not pick up a lot of the sea breeze activity in the summer, and so will not bear much relationship to the conditions you will actually be sailing in. So when you order a report, make sure you know exactly what you are getting.

Forecasting

Meteorological centres are central to the second stage of your weather forecasting job, which is the day by day forecasts you will need at the regatta venue once you are there. Wherever you get it – television, radio, newspaper, or more specialist sources – weather analysis and forecast information comes originally from a meteorological centre. You can get the forecast from one of the people they supply it to for re-publication, i.e. a newspaper, or, and this is becoming more common, you can go direct to the weather centre.

In the same way that newspapers and television and radio stations buy forecast information and pass it on to you as part of their service, you can also buy forecast information directly. Many weather centres have a commercial department that will provide it for you. At a recent One Ton Cup in Cagliari, Sardinia, locally available information was negligible. As a result the hotel reception at 8 a.m. was one long queue of navigators, all waiting to get the weather forecasts that were being faxed in from most of Europe's weather centres. But it is not cheap: it will cost you (1994 prices) in the region of twenty-five US dollars a day to get a personal, faxed-in forecast.

That may not be within your budget, but if it is, it can be money well spent. If you choose the right centre. Meteorological stations form a global network exchanging the raw data of forecasting, taken from local observing stations, and then running this through powerful, computer forecasting programs. The bigger the weather centre the better their computers and programs are likely to be, and the better the quality of the forecast. In Europe the biggest operations are the Bracknell Weather Centre and the European Centre for Medium Range Weather Forecasting. But it is also important to consider whether they can provide you with the kind of forecast that you, as a racing sailor, need. With its small-scale attention to wind direction and all the things; clouds, thermal activity, etc. that affect this.

Because of this some forecasting centres have become specialists in providing regatta forecasts, to the extent that a 'weather van' follows the US big boat circuit around, selling forecasts that are faxed in daily particularly for the regatta venue. For this reason it is not unheard of for a US boat to be using a US forecast centre whilst sailing at a European regatta. The way the stations are inter-linked makes it possible for them to access all the necessary information to give you a good forecast. The advantage of sticking with one centre is that you get to know the people personally and perhaps will have telephone access to them so you can discuss any queries with the forecaster. They also get to know what you need, and once you have faith in someone's performance and judgement it is often better to stick with them wherever you go in the world.

If this is not within your budget then you have several other choices. Your options fall into four categories: forecasts available by fax or phone, television, radio or newspaper. To find out what is available you can refer to the almanac or pilot book, which will almost certainly list local weather forecast sources. You should phone any local weather centre, even if you do not want to buy a forecast, as they will be able to tell you where else you can look. Check with the harbourmaster, marina office, yacht club or chandler as they may well display a forecast, probably from the better of the local sources, on their noticeboard. If they don't, they should be able to tell you where to access the information yourself.

Perhaps the best of these options, also the most expensive, is the fax or phone service set-up for the yachtsman. There has been an explosion in the provision of this kind of service in recent years and most regatta venues will now be covered by the facility. You dial in through a fax or phone and receive either a verbal or printed forecast. The fax versions are particularly good as they allow you to see a good quality weather map, so you can make your own interpretations of the situation. They are generally premium-rated phone services, so they can end up being quite expensive.

Many local radio stations provide regular weather forecasts, on both AM and FM bands. The problem is that it may not be tailored for yachtsmen and may not be that accurate. Again, ask locally if there are any stations which broadcast forecast information particularly for yachtsmen. The other cheap sources of weather information are the television and newspapers. A certain amount of research is usually necessary here, the tendency to provide forecasts with cute graphics of rain clouds rather than the isobars and frontal systems of the original weather map can make them all but useless to the yachtsman. Again, you need to get to the venue early, buy the local papers, watch the TV and see what kind of information they provide.

Personal Observation

Once you have your forecast, the job does not end with blind obedience. Forecasting is not yet a precise science, mainly because the computational power does not yet exist to make it so. It is your job as the racing sailor to interpret what you see, to make best use of the forecast once you are out on the water. This means doing plenty of background reading and plenty of watching the skies, comparing your forecast to what actually happens. Watching the clouds to see what types mean the coming and going of fronts, troughs and ridges is particularly important during the run-up to a regatta. You need to get in tune with the local weather patterns and develop a feel for the accuracy of the forecast that you are using, but, as far as possible, it is something that you should do every day of your life. Your circumstances of work or lifestyle may make this impossible, but if you can it is one of the most worthwhile tasks in regatta preparation. Phillipe Poupon, the French long-distance racer, spends weeks or months before big events studying the weather from the same sources as he will have aboard his boat on the race. Working with Jean-Yves Bernot, the weather routeur, he watches patterns, predicts changes, plots strategies and then assesses how they would have turned out. A high percentage of championships are held during the summer, and understanding how the local conditions are affected by thermal, sea breeze activity is often the key to a successful week. A sound background knowledge of sea-breeze development is essential. Then you need to be watching what happens every day to see whether the early morning conditions of gradient wind, cloud cover, temperature and humidity help or hinder a sea breeze. If you do get a sea breeze how does it develop? At what time and how quickly? What about the direction, does it clock round with the sun consistently or in big jumps at the end of the day? This is the kind of thing that only time at the venue and accurate personal observation can teach you.

However much preparation and forecasting work you do, there is no substitute for keeping your eyes open and watching the skies around you. (*Peter Bentley*)

And it is probably the decisive condition at the majority of big championships. Every serious regatta yachtsman should be an obsessive sea breeze analyst. Take a leaf out of Poupon's book, and apply the same kind of diligence, and you will be well on the way to that crucial top ten, first windward mark position.'

Part 4

Administration

Chapter 9
Logistics

Whilst it sounds almost dramatic in its dullness, running your regatta programme effectively will probably have a more positive impact on the results than buying new sails the week before the event. The following chapter assesses some of the potential pitfalls available to those new to the campaign game.

Entry

It sometimes strikes me, when I see the entry requirements for something like the Admiral's Cup, that they were designed to keep people out of the event, not let them in, so long is the list of hurdles and hoops that must be leapt over and through. For every regatta on your season's programme, and especially the big one that is the culmination of all the rest, you should contact the organising body or club as early as possible. What you are after is the Notice of Race and Entry Form.

Under Part II, Organisation and Management, of the International Yacht Racing Rules the organising authority must publish a Notice of Race (NOR), and Rule 2 of that section describes what it must contain. The NOR is important because it will tell you everything you need to know and possibly take action on prior to arriving at the event. This will include items such as the place and date of the event, the rules, including various class rules that are applicable, conditions and restrictions on entry, the times and requirements for any registration and the time of the first race.

You should go through the Notice of Race carefully; it will explain the parameters of the regatta that you are about to compete in. You are particularly looking for things that you must comply with, either prior to or at the regatta. Check the entry and registration requirements, the closing date and entry fee; do you need anything special such as photos of the crew or insurance certificates? Make sure if you are sponsored that you will comply with the advertising category. Look out for any changes to the class rules, often connected with safety, that may mean additional equipment has to be purchased prior to the regatta – such as a bigger anchor or different lifejackets. It is all too easy to miss items like this and find that the local chandler has (no surprise) just sold out of the items in question, since half the fleet has run into the same problem as you. Poor attention to detail in advance of the regatta can turn apparently minor items into epics as you scour unfamiliar country-side for the required 3kg anchor/fluorescent tape/whistle/etc.

Also look for the measurement requirements. We have already discussed ensuring that your boat is completely legal, now you must make sure you know where to be to pass any scrutineering that is taking place. The NOR should also tell you whether there will be an alternative penalty rule in place – will you need an 'I' flag? The courses to be sailed should be listed; see if this includes anything unusual such as a list of navigational marks that you need to know about. It is from this section that you should be able to make your chart purchase and begin your research on the race course sailing water.

Reproduced below is the NOR from a recent J24 British National Championship. At the bottom is included a list of notes and pointers that might be made from it as part of your regatta preparation. Armed with this information you should be able to complete successfully both the entry form prior to the event and registration once you get there.

Travel

We have already discussed the precautions involved in ensuring the boat gets to the venue in one piece and ready for action. You must also think about getting you and your crew there in the best possible state for the coming challenge. Whilst I have seen people arrive at events by hitch-hiking and private jet, your most likely methods are by car and perhaps ferry, a commercial flight or some other means of public transport such as a bus or train. Obviously the distance is central to the question of how you approach travelling to the regatta. If the venue is just a couple of hours down the road you are unlikely to need much planning to get you there in one piece. But driving half-way across Europe to Cadiz or Athens from the UK requires some advance thinking, particularly if you have not done it before.

There are two approaches when tackling your travel plans: you can either get there as quickly as you can regardless of the potential discomfort and then have a day or two to recover when you arrive, or you can take your time, and arrive ready to start work. Most people seem to prefer getting there as quickly as possible, something to do with the pace of modern life I suppose. The danger is to

13.   The intended programme for the event is as follows:

Sat 27 Aug	0845-2000		Registration & Measurement
Sun 28 Aug	0845-1200 1400		Registration & Measurement Race 1
Mon 29 Aug	1100 asap after	: :	Race 2 Race 3
Tue 30 Aug	1100 asap after	: :	Race 4 Race 5
Wed 31 Aug	1030 asap after 1800-1930	: : :	Race 6 (Reserve Race) Class AGM in Clubhouse
Thu 01 Sep	1030 asap after 1930 for 2000	: : :	Race 7 (Reserve Race) Prizegiving Dinner/Disco

14.   The completed entry form and entry fee must be posted to the UK J/24 Class Association Secretary no later than Monday 25 July 1994. The postmark will be regarded as proof of posting. No acknowledgement of entries will be made. Late entries will be accepted up to and including Monday 22 August 1994 with an additional late entry fee of £25.00.

Return to: Jackie Barker
                   UK J/24 Class Association
                   105 Magdalen Road
                   London
                   SW18 3NW
                   Tel: 081 875 9566

15.   All parties involved in the organisation and the running of this event shall not accept any liability for any accident, injury, damage or loss of personal material or otherwise to yachts, third parties and participants before, during or after the Championships.

The Notice of Race from the UK Open J24 National Championship 1994, hosted by the Royal Lymington Yacht Club and reproduced with their permission. The following are notes that might be made on receiving such a NOR, the numbers refer to the paragraphs on the notice.

Notes

1. Need charts and tide tables for Christchurch Bay and West Solent.
6. Check class membership/find card.
7. Phone crew and organise target weights, plus a check weigh session.

---

13.   The intended programme for the event is as follows:

Sat 27 Aug	0845-2000		Registration & Measurement
Sun 28 Aug	0845-1200 1400		Registration & Measurement Race 1
Mon 29 Aug	1100 asap after	: :	Race 2 Race 3
Tue 30 Aug	1100 asap after	: :	Race 4 Race 5
Wed 31 Aug	1030 asap after 1800-1930	: : :	Race 6 (Reserve Race) Class AGM in Clubhouse
Thu 01 Sep	1030 asap after 1930 for 2000	: : :	Race 7 (Reserve Race) Prizegiving Dinner/Disco

14.   The completed entry form and entry fee must be posted to the UK J/24 Class Association Secretary no later than Monday 25 July 1994. The postmark will be regarded as proof of posting. No acknowledgement of entries will be made. Late entries will be accepted up to and including Monday 22 August 1994 with an additional late entry fee of £25.00.

Return to: Jackie Barker
                    UK J/24 Class Association
                    105 Magdalen Road
                    London
                    SW18 3NW
                    Tel: 081 875 9566

15.   All parties involved in the organisation and the running of this event shall not accept any liability for any accident, injury, damage or loss of personal material or otherwise to yachts, third parties and participants before, during or after the Championships.

Need everybody ready to weigh in at registration – 27th August 08.45
8. Find measurement certificate. Check required/optional equipment and do inventory. Put copy on board.
9. Phone sailmaker and arrange pick up for new jib, phone measurer regards getting jib measured, plus all sails check measured.
11. Check insurance
12. Organise crew meeting for dates and travel to venue – registration 27/8 and first race 28/8
14. Send entry form in.

arrive without leaving sufficient time to get the travelling out of your system. Along with a lot of the rest of your preparation the time you can allow will depend on your circumstances, but the more time you have at the venue the better off you will be. At least up to a point; there certainly comes a time when you just get sick of it all and want to go home and lead a 'normal life'. I've seen this malaise set in to a lot of people who set off around Europe for months of training and regattas, living out of the back of an estate car. But if your trip is two or three weeks it should not be a problem.

We have already talked about the mechanical preparations involved in trailing your boat to the regatta. The next thing to tackle is the logistics. Which route are you going to take? You can ask this question of the motoring organisations, like the RAC and the AA in the UK, who provide this as a service. They will work out a recommended route for you, though this can go wrong. I know one story where a large keelboat and Range Rover arrived at the foot of one of the steepest hills in the UK with the brakes on fire, and that was on a road the AA had recommended him to take.

Mostly, a good map and some common sense will enable you to figure it out for yourself. The parameters as always are time and money. Sticking the boat and trailer on a ferry for twenty-four hours is often the least stressful way to complete a journey, but it is also more expensive than driving for twenty hours and spending only four on the ferry. The same problem arises when tackling motorway networks which are tolled. Again it can add to the cost of the journey to use toll roads, but it considerably reduces the time taken and the hassle encountered. You have to decide whether the time saved outweighs the extra cost, and this will depend on your circumstances.

Once you have planned your route, book any ferries that you have decided to take well in advance. Ferries can fill up, particularly in holiday periods, and your boat and trailer combination will need a fair amount of space. As we have already mentioned, make sure the car and trailer are serviced and in a fit state to complete the journey. You also need to check the legal aspects, particularly if you are driving abroad. The people to ask are the motoring organisations; they will be able to tell you about differing legal requirements for the countries you will be travelling in. Examples are insurance, whether your licence is valid, things you must carry (like warning triangles) and things you must not (petrol cans). You should also take out breakdown insurance, which will get you and the boat home when all else (like the rear axle) fails. You should also check that the car is insured to tow a trailer, and that the boat is insured while it is being towed. If the regatta is abroad then make sure that the boat is also covered whilst it is being raced in another country.

It is easy to think you can skimp on this stuff, and even if you are the type who would risk going on holiday without insurance cover, you should think twice before taking the chance on a regatta trip. Writing off the car on the way to a European regatta and then discovering you were not insured is one guaranteed way to get a bad result. Confidently taking a new car on a two thousand mile road trip, only to miss the regatta because it broke down and you had not bothered with breakdown insurance, is another way to waste all that careful regatta preparation on a simple detail.

Medical insurance, along with general travel insurance for belongings, money and tickets, is an absolute must. Even within the European Union facilities are not necessarily reciprocated and they certainly will not extend to repatriating you by air ambulance if the worst should happen. But check that the policy does not specifically exclude sailing, or competitive sport – some of them do.

If you are taking public or commercial transport much the same applies. Book in advance and think about the route carefully. How close is the airport to the venue? How are you going to get there? If money is an issue you don't want a cab ride that costs nearly as much as the flight because you have not figured out how to get from one to the other. If you are carrying large amounts of gear it is always worth getting to the terminal, be it bus, train or particularly airline, early. Excess baggage tends to be taken on a first-come-first-served basis, and if you arrive late they may not have room. The other option is to phone in advance, particularly with over-size objects, so that they are expecting you. You also get a better seat choice if you check in early, particularly important if you are travelling economy and going any distance.

Wherever you are going abroad do not forget to check on the visa requirements, both for your final destination and any countries you are transiting. Your travel agent should be able to tell you about the requirements. In all types of travelling the important thing is not to succumb to the boredom and discomfort of it all and resort to gorging on food or alcohol. This is particularly difficult to adhere to on international flights when the alcohol is so free-flowing, but it is the worst thing you can do if you want to arrive in good shape. Aircraft interiors dehydrate you badly at the best of times, and alcohol only makes it worse. There is also no point destroying all the careful diet, weight control and fitness programme by sitting cramped in the back of the car gorging sugar-laden food and drink for two days without exercise. Do not rely on service stations to provide a reasonable or balanced diet. Try to take good food with you – fruit, nuts, juice drinks, cheese and biscuits. Take whatever you can carry and keep, and stay away from the junk food. Instant gratification of those urges will only result in feeling terrible later on.

And this comes back to the earlier point about arriving in better health if you take your time. Doing the journey in two eight-hour stints with a stop for some decent food, a good night's sleep and some exercise will get you there in infinitely better shape than a sixteen-hour, chocolate- and caffeine-fuelled blitz. But it also gets you there a day later and a night's accommodation poorer – you pays your money and you takes your choice.

Accommodation

In an ideal world we would all fly first-class to the venue and get picked up by the boat captain who had arrived a couple of weeks earlier, then check in to the nearest five star hotel and after a good night's sleep join the crew and boat who are sitting at the dock waiting for the first prac- tice sail. Unfortunately reality is a little different, and all too often we end up in a soaking wet tent or in the back of the car. And I speak as someone who has done it both ways.

But whatever your budget I think there are some defi- nite do's and don't's when it comes to accommodation, the most important of which is that you have to have a good night's sleep if you are at all serious about getting a result at the event. If you cannot afford, or organise, decent accommodation, which means a real bed and roof over your head, then you would be better not to go. Or at least go for the experience, the adventure, the fun, whatever, but don't kid yourself you are going to be competitive. Unless you are exceptionally talented or the opposition is partic- ularly hopeless, or all doing the same thing.

The second comment is that the cheap-looking option often doesn't turn out to be so cheap. It is all too easy to decide to camp or sleep in the van rather than splash out on the self-catering apartment, and then end up spending a fortune in the bar or restaurant because the tent is too cold/wet/miserable to spend any time in, never mind do anything as ambitious as cook. Be practical when you are approaching this problem. It is a lot cheaper and preferable to cook for yourself and have somewhere comfortable to relax in the evening than ending up in a restaurant or eating junk food all week.

Assuming that you do have the budget to book accommodation from a reasonable range of choice there are other factors you should consider. The priority I always think of is to be near the boat park or marina. This need grows exponentially in importance with increasing number of crew and decreasing amount of transport. If everyone can make their own way to the boat in the morning, by foot, bike or car, then it considerably reduces the amount of hassle involved. There is no co-ordinating to be done. No waiting around for those who are late, or do not need to be at the boat early, until the transport can leave. You simply need a time at which everyone should be at the boat with their responsibilities covered and everything ready to go. If someone has to be there two hours early to fix something or scrub the bottom it does not need major logistical planning to make it happen. So try to get accommodation close to the boat.

A further aspect of this is where you can keep the spares and tools that you need close to the boat. Security is a big aspect of this and if your flat or hotel is a hundred yards from the boat it solves the problem. If you can then find secure parking for the week and just leave the car there, empty, do so; it is one less thing to worry about. Other options will depend on how bad the security problem is in that area. Driving in to the boat each day then leaving spares, tools etc. in the car is one possibility, but this can be risky. There are stories in the Mediterranean of everything being stripped from cars which their owners had left for a couple of minutes to ask directions at the yacht club to their accommodation. It is a reasonable principle to act as though this will happen until you discover otherwise. Do not leave a vehicle unattended with anything in it until you have had a chance to ask the locals, or sailors who have arrived there before you, what the deal is.

At one European circuit regatta virtually the only person not to get their car stripped, usually overnight parked outside the accommodation, was the guy who had broken down en route to the venue and then checked it into a garage for the week to get it fixed for the trip home. If you are somewhere like this and the accommodation is too far away and/or you have too much spare kit to cart backwards and forwards from the flat every day, then it is probably better to leave it in the boat than in the car. Often dinghy parks are guarded at least overnight or twenty-four hours a day in high-risk areas. During the day piling it under the covers out of sight is the traditional and reasonably secure option. Thieves are after your stereo, cash or other valuables, which are all good reasons to break into a car. Once in they may take your tools or sailing kit if nothing else presents itself, but they are much less likely to go rootling around under a boat cover looking for that kind of stuff. Building a secure box that will hold everything and will fix on to the trailer, but detachable so you can dump it beside the boat for the week, is the best option after leaving spares in nearby accommodation. You should also ask, when booking accommodation, if there is secure parking, perhaps underground. Getting the car trashed half-way through the week, or worse, before a final crucial race, is a distraction you do not need. If you can afford the kind of accommodation that means this sort of thing is no longer a worry, go for it.

Assuming you have the budget to choose, the decision between self-catering and hotel is a difficult one. If you have a 'support team' (this may just be a euphemism for non-sailing partner in attendance) they might be willing to cook for the week. I think this is the best option as it allows complete control over diet and when you eat. The problem with restaurants is limited control over the type of food you eat, booking them, particularly if you are in a resort area in the summer when they will be busy, and the fact that a restaurant meal can take a couple of hours. You may enjoy that method of relaxing in the evening, but not everyone in the crew necessarily will. A home-cooked meal that can be done and dusted in half an hour allows everyone the freedom to choose their own form of entertainment for the rest of the evening. However, if the sailors must cook, it is a difficult choice between the downsides of the restaurant, and the concerns of cooking – doing the shopping, which can be difficult enough if you are on the water all day, never mind stirring yourself to cook after a long, hard day on the water.

Finally, whatever you do, make sure it is sorted out well in advance. Turning up at the venue and hoping to find somewhere is a good way to end up spending a couple of nights in the back of the car and the rest of the regatta distracted. The disadvantage with booking in advance is not knowing exactly what you are getting until you get there. This is particularly true of self-catering accommodation, which is rarely the subject of the scrutiny and checking that guidebooks and the star system provide for hotels.

The propensity of agents to describe their charge in rather glowing terms does not help either. If you can find somebody who has been there before, or perhaps phone your national authority if it is a venue that is regularly used for regattas, and get a recommendation, do so.

Ideally you would probably go on a reconnaissance mission to check it out and book the accommodation months before the event. But this is not within everyone's budget and even then it can go wrong. I went on one such mission for a yacht regatta and the place, a couple of apartments in a holiday park, looked fine, particularly in view of our rather limited campaign budget. When we came back three months later it was in the middle of the summer and the place was full of screaming kids by day and hormonally charged night-clubbing teenagers by night. The walls were paper thin and no one got any sleep all week. We didn't win, and it was the first time we had been beaten all season. If you can afford to spend the money on decent accommodation, do so.

Sailing Instructions

Once you are at the venue, settled into your comfortable accommodation, the boat safely set up and sorted out and a couple of days sailing under your belt, you should start to think more closely about the racing itself. The first thing you need is the sailing instructions. It may tell you in the Notice of Race where and when these are to be acquired. The normal practice is to issue them on registration of entry. Once you have them you need to find yourself somewhere quiet for an hour or so and sit down with a rule book and a pen to read them.

You are unlikely to have got as far in sailing as to want to read this book, without having come across sailing instructions or the rule book. And you will know why you need both together, unless of course you can remember the rules by heart. Personally I am always much happier if I have thumbed through the book and checked out all the references and modifications. I have seen sailing instructions vary from a page to twenty pages, depending on the nature of the regatta (and, if I dare say it, on the nature of the race committee). But you are always looking for the same basic points.

1. What is the start line constituted by, and what is the sequence of classes (if there is more than one) and guns? This should include both individual and general recall procedures, and how your start is timed after a general recall is signalled.
2. What is the course, and if there is more than one how are they going to tell you which course it is?
3. What and where is the finishing line?
4. Can they change or shorten the course, and if so how and where can it be done?
5. Do you need to sign, or declare, at the beginning or end of each race, on or off the water?
6. Are there any alternative penalties in force?
7. What is the protest procedure?

If you can extract and memorise these points from the instructions you are in pretty good shape. You should also note anything in the instructions that you need to act on. Do you need any other flags, a declaration form and so on. This stuff should have been predictable from the Notice of Race, but check the SIs anyway. Personally I always like to carry the instructions, suitably waterproofed, on board the boat. You cannot memorise every detail and if you are unsure of something, a flag or unusual procedure, it is nice to have the instructions, along with a rule book and flag chart, to hand. Obviously you may not want all this stuff on a light dinghy, but anything bigger I think can justify the weight.

One final aspect of international regattas is language. If the regatta is a genuinely international affair, a World Championship or circuit regatta perhaps, then English must be the definitive language. This is an IYRU rule; discrepancies between sets of instructions will be decided upon interpretation of the English version. So if you are going to a World Championship you need no more than a knowledge of English. If you are going to a national championship of a country where English is not the first language you had better pack a dictionary, know the language or have someone around who does, because there is no reason for them to provide anything other than the national language version. But if it is a Worlds and the committee is attempting to make another language version the over-riding one, then they are in the wrong and you are perfectly within your rights to insist on the English version.

When It Is All Over

Preparation for the next regatta starts as soon as the last one finishes, and you should always spend some time on debriefing. The most important aspect after every regatta is to analyse how you matched up to your goals. Did you achieve what you wanted to, and if not why not? You must then feed this back into your training programme, whether it is mid- season or the final event of the year and the one that all your preparation has been about.

Concentrate on your goals, but think through everything else as well, to see what is to be learnt. Getting better is all about not repeating your mistakes. And the best way to do this is to be clear about what they were. Break down each aspect of the regatta and note down what you learned. How was the boat, write down the settings that were successful. Did you learn anything about boat tune, or see any ideas for gear on other boats that you want to try out? Did you have any gear failure, if so why; where was your preparation lacking in this department? How did the crew work figure out? Were you fit enough, was the boat handling all right? How did you work as a team? Do you need to make changes?

Then there is the venue. What do you know, what would you tell yourself before you went back? Does the tide or current behave as advertised, are there anomalies? What about the wind; does the place have a reputation for one particular condition? If so, is it really like that? Does the beat pay one way consistently; if so, which way? Write down everything you wish you had known at the start of the week, the answers to all the questions you were asking then. Because although the most important lessons are to be learned within the goal structure of the programme, there is still a tremendous amount of information that you can note down for the future. This is the reconnaissance trip for the next regatta at this venue. So don't just concentrate on the race-course, think about whether you met anyone who had a better deal on the accommodation than you. If there was, what was the address and phone number so you can book it next time? The same thing with restaurants, the travel arrangements, the sailing club, chandlers, weather forecast and so on. Note down and keep it all. The next time you race there you will be twice as well prepared.

Index